Reading the First Five Books

Reading the First Five Books

THE INVITATION OF THE PENTATEUCH'S STORIES

Rachel Toombs

Baker Academic
a division of Baker Publishing Group
Grand Rapids, Michigan

Published by Baker Academic
a division of Baker Publishing Group
Grand Rapids, Michigan
BakerAcademic.com

Printed in the United States of America

Library of Congress Cataloging-in-Publication Data
Names: Toombs, Rachel, author.
Title: Reading the first five books : the invitation of the pentateuch's stories / Rachel Toombs.
Description: Grand Rapids, Michigan : Baker Academic, a division of Baker Publishing Group, [2024] | Includes bibliographical references and index.
Identifiers: LCCN 2024002306 | ISBN 9781540965905 (paperback) | ISBN 9781540968463 (casebound) | ISBN 9781493448388 (ebook) | ISBN 9781493448395 (pdf)
Subjects: LCSH: Bible. Pentateuch—Criticism, interpretation, etc. | Storytelling—Religious aspects—Christianity.
Classification: LCC BS1225.52 .T6555 2024 | DDC 222/.106—dc23/eng/20240423
LC record available at https://lccn.loc.gov/2024002306

Cover design by Paula Gibson
Cover art: Illuminated page from Genesis, manuscript 18 folio 1 verso / DeAgostini / Superstock

Baker Publishing Group publications use paper produced from sustainable forestry practices and postconsumer waste whenever possible.

24 25 26 27 28 29 30 7 6 5 4 3 2 1

To Eileen and Doug Toombs,
the first to invite me to wonder and wander through stories

Contents

PREFACE

In March 2020, I found myself confronted with the challenges of shifting both my parish and my university teaching from in-person to remote learning. With dread and inexperience, I moved uncomfortably into the online space. I was *sure* this would diminish the "magic" of communal learning and be a season to suffer through rather than embrace. Of course, I was right that much of the pandemic was far from ideal and brought many challenges. I shifted my seminar-style class to a truncated online weekly call with discussion boards to supplement the lack of in-person engagement. For my church work, I desired to retain some sense of normalcy amid major upheaval. Here we were, journeying through Lent toward Holy Week and the joy of Easter Sunday, siloed each to our own couches and makeshift desks, clinging to community across computer screens. Our parish quickly began an online Bible study at Holy Spirit Episcopal Church in Waco, Texas. Young, old, and all in between gathered together each Sunday morning to read through one of the narratives of the lectionary reading for that day. I expected these online gatherings to be a sorry substitute for the parish hall. What I found, though, was that the desire for connection and the time to sit with the text invited deep and meaningful conversation. We had undistracted time each week to read slowly and wonder what God might be doing through the stories of Ezekiel's vision of dry bones, Jacob's wrestling with a mysterious man in the middle of the night, and Jesus's cryptic parables. We wondered together about how Ezekiel's vision might have looked, how Jacob might have felt, how we are invited to stand with the crowd listening to Jesus with wonder and confusion.

The idea for this book began then, as I realized that the invitation to read can be offered even through buffering videos, awkward camera angles, and accidentally clicking the mute button. I watched as those I invited to wonder and wander through the text began to attune to Scripture in a new way, seeing the challenging bits of the text as an opportunity to dig deeper. I discovered through this experience that part of my job, my vocation, as a teacher—in the parish or in the classroom—is to serve as a kind of scriptural host by extending the invitation of reading. When I returned to in-person teaching, now at St. Alban's Episcopal Church in Waco, I carried this posture of invitation with me. I am grateful and fortunate to be entrusted to teach these two special parishes deep in the heart of Texas by the Rev. Jason Ingalls and the Rev. Aaron M. G. Zimmerman.

I knew how to extend this invitation because I have been formed by those who taught me to take up and read. It is to that great company that I want to offer my thanks for this book. Thank you to my parents, Eileen and Doug Toombs, and my youth minister, Scott Volltrauer. Thank you to those who opened up the wide world of biblical studies with historical, theological, literary, and linguistic ways to wander through the text: Gary Long, Pamela Erwin, Carl Rasmussen, and Michael Holmes of Bethel University (St. Paul, MN); Iain Provan, Phil Long, and David Clemens of Regent College (Vancouver, BC); and Bill Bellinger and Jim Nogalski of Baylor University (Waco, TX). I have many others to thank, including those who read drafts, offered comments, or tolerated my random thoughts as I formulated this book, including Gisela Kreglinger, Amanda Brobst-Renaud, Lacy Crocker Papadakis, and Stephanie Drum. Special thanks to my editor, Jim Kinney, and copyeditor, Melisa Blok, at Baker Academic: Jim for helping me to discover the shape of this book and for encouraging my voice as a teacher to come through in my writing; Melisa for making my writing look better than it deserves.

Finally, I want to thank two people to whom I owe so much that these passing lines feel completely insufficient. Thank you Rebecca Poe Hays, my friend, writing partner, and great encourager. I could not have dreamed up, begun, continued, or completed this book without you. And thank you Lance Green; I love you. Life would be so much harder and less joyful without you by my side.

INTRODUCTION

> Blessed Lord, who hast caused all holy Scriptures to be written for our learning: Grant that we may in such wise hear them, read, mark, learn, and inwardly digest them; that, by patience and comfort of thy holy Word, we may embrace and ever hold fast the blessed hope of everlasting life, which thou hast given us in our Savior Jesus Christ; who liveth and reigneth with thee and the Holy Spirit, one God, for ever and ever. *Amen.*
>
> *The Book of Common Prayer* (1979, p. 184)

I remember being introduced to the spiritual practice of *lectio divina* in undergrad. This slow and meditative reading of a small portion of Scripture, a practice rooted in the rich monastic tradition of contemplative prayer, transformed how I thought about reading the Bible. Amid cramming for an upcoming Old Testament history exam, and surrounded by stacks of notecards filled with ancient Near Eastern rulers and key dates, I found this exercise of slowly reading to be a balm to my weary mind and anxiety-ridden soul. Scripture was something that could be savored and that could serve as an invitation into a space of prayer, honest self-reflection, and confession. Years later, I was introduced to the evocative prayer of Thomas Cranmer, where he asks that God give us ears to hear, eyes to read, hands to mark, and minds to be transformed through our reading of Scripture. There is something shared between the monastic practice of *lectio divina* and Cranmer's prayer for patience and comfort in our reading of Scripture: a conviction that Scripture not only instructs but invites us into prayerful encounters with the living God.

Similarly, Catholic novelist Flannery O'Connor writes that "a story is a way to say something that can't be said any other way, and it takes every word in the story to say what the meaning is. You tell a story because a statement would be inadequate. When anybody asks what a story is about, the only proper thing is to tell him to read the story."[1] We do not read stories merely for factual knowledge. Stories cannot be replaced by abstract principles, bulleted lists, or CliffsNotes versions. Propositional statements and overviews have their useful place, but there is only one way to know what a story is about—and that is to read it. Even the central creedal claims of the Christian faith are storied in their proclamations; we believe in a God who creates, incarnates, sends, and redeems. For example, we know God is a creator God because the early chapters of Genesis narrate the creation of the world, not once but with two evocative stories. We are not simply told that God creates the world but shown it through an unfolding drama. We also come to know the character of God as creator through these early chapters; God creates by making order of chaos, creating spaces that God then fills with creatures and other living things that will thrive in them, and all along God delights in this creative work. To know the Christian story, then, is also to take up and read. Stories invite us as readers into the work of meaning-making in a unique way.

This book centers on the invitation to read the first five books of the Bible, called the Pentateuch in the Christian tradition and the Torah in the Hebrew tradition. These books mark the beginning of both the Hebrew Bible and the Christian Scriptures.[2] An invitation to read entails being caught up in the story, the artistry of the biblical narrative. An invitation, in the spirit of Cranmer, to be transformed through reading the Holy Writ.

From the genesis of the world to final preparations to enter the land promised to Abraham's descendants, the Pentateuch speaks of the cosmic and quotidian primarily through storytelling. In some places, storytelling is replaced by other kinds of tellings, including genealogies, instructions, songs, and summaries; but these other genre types stand in contrast to the general narrative thrust of not only the first five books but Scripture

1. O'Connor, *Mystery and Manners*, 96.

2. In this book, I will be speaking about the Old Testament as the older of the two testaments of Christian Scripture. While I am approaching the text as a Christian reader, it is also important to note that the Old Testament was first (and remains) the Hebrew Bible for the Jewish community, who received, shaped, maintained, and used this religious text.

as a whole. Stories really seem to matter in conveying who God is, who we are, and our proper relationship to both God and those around us. If O'Connor is right (and I think she is) when she says that "a story is a way to say something that can't be said any other way" and that the only suitable way to know what a story is about is to read it, then it seems that an important part of the life of faith involves being good readers of Scripture.

In this book, I invite readers into the imaginative and transformative work of the stories we find in Scripture's first five books by looking to three general features of bare-bones narration: brevity, pacing, and characterization. We will also look at two more narrow but intriguing aspects of biblical Hebrew: complexity in characterization and the use of the grotesque. Brevity represents the general quality of biblical Hebrew narrative in the Pentateuch, while pacing and characterization are less frequent, but notable, features of Hebrew stories. I show through these explorations how the spare quality of Hebrew narrative invites readers into a challenging, fruitful, and risky engagement with these theologically rich stories.

I wrote this book to function as a training ground in a certain way of reading Old Testament narratives. The five chapters on narrative features are structured similarly: I first help to identify one of the literary devices and demonstrate how each device creates opportunities for expanded interpretations of a story. Then, I move to a brief case study demonstrating how this device functions in a biblical story. In chapter 7, we will end our study with an exploration of how the stories of the Pentateuch become foundational for the identity of ancient Israel and the Christian church by looking at how stories are retold throughout Deuteronomy. This final chapter will take a different shape than the others as we look to a number of the key stories that offer ancient Israelites identity and hope for the future.

The primary goal of this book is pedagogical. That is, I do not aim simply to inform you that brevity, pacing, characterization, complexity in characterization, and aspects of the grotesque exist in the Pentateuch. Instead, I want to teach you how to take up these tools and read the text in new and profound ways. I think it is important to lay out a theory of interpretation, or a hermeneutic, that recognizes the active role of readers in meaning-making, because readers must first accept the invitation.

I do this work in chapter 1, "The Invitation of Reading." I characterize my interpretive approach as an invitation into a conversation between the text and the reader. This approach involves a theological account of the importance of stories and the participatory nature of reading that places readers at the center not only of interpretation of Scripture but of encounter with God.

In chapter 2, "Brevity," I explore one of the most distinctive features of biblical Hebrew narrative: its spare style. With the rare exception (e.g., the Joseph novella in Gen. 37–52), the stories in the Pentateuch are told with succinct prose. Some of its most important stories are told with a brevity that can be unsettling. How are we to understand the artistic impulse of such brief stories? Is brevity simply the way of primitive storytelling in the ancient Near East? In this chapter, I show how the brevity of Hebrew narratives serves as an invitation to wonder, to probe, and to question. I close this chapter with a case study on the story of Nadab and Abihu (Lev. 10:1–7).

In chapter 3, I introduce readers to the pacing of biblical Hebrew narrative. In addition to the narrative's spare quality, when we recognize the rapid pace of narration at key moments, it allows for richer engagement and more attention to the artistry of the storytelling. The syntax drives us as readers deeper into the stories. The story of Jacob's wrestling on the banks of Peniel serves as a masterful example of the use of pacing in biblical Hebrew narrative.

I explore characterization in chapter 4. Characterization in literature encompasses all the tools a narrator uses to convey how to understand a story's characters. The spare quality of biblical narrative makes action and dialogue the central and vital ways we understand the actors in a story. We as readers must attend to these indirect modes of characterization to move beyond a flat reading of a biblical story. Examples of indirect characterization are abundant in the first five books of the Old Testament. In fact, nearly every instance of understanding a person in the text comes by way of action or dialogue, and the narratives contain minimal direct description of a figure's appearance, motivations, or character. One of the most fascinating examples of the payoff of this characterization can be found in the obtuse and theologically profound characterization of God in Exodus. By looking to the paradoxical (a burning bush *and* a dark cloud) and enigmatic (Zipporah's seemingly bizarre response to God's threat) characterizations, we find in Exodus both an intimate and an interpretively challenging picture of the God of Abraham, Isaac, and Jacob, who liberates a people and calls them to be his own.

In chapter 5, I delve more deeply into characterization by focusing on one of its subsets: complexity. Complexity in characterization captures the ways a narrative can appear to be overtly casting a character in a particularly good or bad light, even though the narrative in fact offers clues that challenge—and even reverse—the initial depiction of a figure or figures in the story. Readers must attend to how narratives play on our own assumptions and other characters to make subtle, surprising, and sometimes damning critiques. Complexity often appears when we have more than two characters in a narrative. In these narratives with more complex social dynamics, readers can find the narrative's characterization of individuals playing on one another, which requires us to pay attention to interpersonal dynamics to decide who is the hero or the villain of a story. In this chapter, we turn to Genesis 27, where readers encounter four direct speakers rather than the usual two. This allows readers more interpretive opportunities to inhabit the story and to wonder about the dynamics at play during this familial upheaval.

In chapter 6, I move to the gory nature of the Pentateuch, and of the older testament more broadly. I explore how violence and grotesque description reflect both the reality of the human condition and how God works mysteriously through the created order. We will turn to Numbers 16, where we find the story of a group of leaders who rebel against Moses and Aaron's leadership and are swallowed up into the realm of death with their eyes still wide open. My hope for this chapter is to cultivate a confidence in approaching even the sticky bits of Scripture as an invitation to explore these texts rather than be overwhelmed or repulsed by them.

In chapter 7, I reflect on the book of Deuteronomy, which serves both as a distinctive book of the Pentateuch in terms of storytelling—Deuteronomy contains the least amount of narrative of the five—and as a book that models how the stories are meant to be taken up again and again, to be read, remembered, and reinterpreted to recall both who God has been and who God continues to be for ancient Israel. Moses teaches an important lesson: the porous nature of these stories allows room for the subsequent generations to take up these stories again and again in ways that do not exhaust their meaning.

My hope is that this work serves as a call back to the ancient conviction that stories transform readers. We see this conviction at work in the bare-bones style of biblical Hebrew narrative, where the elusive and spare quality of the stories is meant to invite readers into their own wrestling with stories of God and the world. Biblical Hebrew narrative offers, through its artistry, abundant opportunities to wonder and wander as we read. Let us accept the invitation and dig in.

CHAPTER 1

The Invitation of Reading

Introduction

Reading biblical narrative is challenging. Not limited to any one testament, biblical stories confront readers with ancient references told in perplexing styles. Preachers, faced with the violence of humanity across the narrative and a lack of clarity in Jesus's parables, often engage in interpretive gymnastics to get out of the discomfort, and, rather than inviting their parishioners into the text, invite them out of it. This strategy often results in distancing their audiences from peculiar stories that present truths—at times uncomfortable and at others utterly confounding. Quite simply, it would be quite a bit easier to be good readers of Scripture if the stories themselves weren't so frequently elusive in character.

In the early and medieval church, we find recourse to spiritual readings, particularly of the older testament, as a way of overcoming some of its interpretive challenges. The exemplary case of this kind of reading is found in Origen of Alexandria, who believed that all of Scripture contained within its subject matter what was edifying and necessary for the Christian life. While this material can sometimes be found on the literal level of the Old Testament text, there are times when he finds nothing beneficial or sensible on first appearances; thus a deeper and spiritual meaning must be found hidden within the bare letter, much like a kernel within a husk.[1]

1. This kind of allegorical reading of the Hebrew Bible/Old Testament was not limited to Christians. A few hundred years before Origen we find a similar reading strategy in Philo of

Through a spiritual reading, Origen and many Christian readers that follow his example recognize these sticky bits of the text as opportunities to delve below the surface to find hidden spiritual meanings available to them through the revelation of Jesus Christ.

A great wealth of theological insight is found in these kinds of spiritual readings. I do not wish to dismiss in any way the great richness of this interpretive tradition or the conviction that multivalent meanings can be found in Scripture. I do, though, want to state up front that the reading I propose in this book—the invitation of reading biblical Hebrew narrative—should not be confused with these spiritual readings. What I offer in the following pages is the invitation not to get below the "bare letter" or literal level of the text, as we see in spiritual readings like those of Origen. On the other side, I do not wish to get behind the text to human authorial intention or "what really happened," as is the tendency of some biblical scholars. While I see value in both approaches, I aim in this work to help invite readers into the world of the narrative. To wander around, as it were, and wonder about why the stories are told the way they are. In the following chapters, we will wander and wonder about many stories in the Pentateuch. But first, in order to understand this readerly invitation, I think it best to take a step back and ask ourselves what it even means to approach texts as a reader.

Hermeneutics as Invitation

Most of us take for granted that we come to a text, including the text you are currently reading, and derive meaning from the words on a page. Some of us might *not* take for granted that others can look at a great work of art or read a stanza of poetry and derive meaning from something seemingly less obvious to the rest of us. The study of meaning-making, of interpreting texts and other created works, falls under the umbrella of "hermeneutics." In the simplest of terms, hermeneutics seeks to make sense of how we appropriate meaning (i.e., interpret) from any given ob-

Alexandria, among others. Both of these figures are part of the larger Alexandrian School, which was largely influenced by the Platonic and Neoplatonic traditions. In his *On First Principles*, Origen refers to instances when the literal level offers readers nothing of spiritual benefit as "stumbling blocks or interruptions of the narratival sense," which cause the reader to seek out a hidden spiritual meaning in the text. Origen, *On First Principles* 4.2.9 (2:515).

ject. More elaborately: "Hermeneutics is sometimes understood as an art practiced by every human being engaging in social interactions, sometimes as a discipline of the humanities that builds on that art and elaborates explicit rules, sometimes as that discipline's philosophical justification. . . . Its basic operation is not explanation, as in the natural sciences, but understanding."[2] Hermeneutics aims to identify how we ascribe meaning to words on a page, colors on a canvas, or anything else that requires some kind of mediation (which is most things!).

I am an avid baker. When looking for a new recipe, I frequently scour the comments section of a food blog. The ingredients list and instructions can tell me quite a bit about what I will make and whether it will be an absolute disaster (say, the proportions appear way off or the oven is set to an unreasonable temperature). What the list of ingredients does not tell me is if this is an exceptionally good recipe. I go to the comments section, not the ingredient list, to know if the baked treat will actually taste good. In other words, there is a difference between raw data and end products. Of course, I need to know how many cups of flour to add and when to add them, but that is not *why* I am baking: I bake for the tasty treat, not the unmixed ingredients. There is always the danger that one of the commentors may prove an inadequate baker or that I may mistake the sugar for the salt and end up with something far from the intent of the food blogger. The possibility of mistake is inevitable because the recipe will not bake itself. It requires that I am involved in the making. In a way, this is also how we come to make meaning—we cannot be aloof observers but rather are involved in any kind of meaning-making. And being involved means we run the risk of making a mess of things. But it also means that we might improve on the recipe or riff on it in a way that leads to something new and exciting, something that the original food blogger did not anticipate. This baking event, including my missteps and ingenuity, are all part of the interpretive act, where the recipe as text and myself as reader meet to make meaning via a tasty treat.

As an example, consider the wilderness wanderings that mark a large portion of the Pentateuch from the middle of Exodus through the close of Deuteronomy. I grew up in Minnesota, where just as one season is getting too long we get a hint of the weather changing, with snow melting or cooler nights, the leaves budding or turning to vibrant hues of yellow

2. Hösle, "Hermeneutics," 618.

and orange. When I first moved to Texas, I arrived in mid-June. I had previously thought of this time of year as the *start* of summer, but when I arrived in central Texas, I felt like the summer inferno was already in full swing. I remember looking forward to September and the coming of fall, only to be sorely disappointed when the heat just . . . persisted. After my first couple summers, I learned to anticipate the long slog of heat, sun, mosquitoes, and scorched earth. I also found that I began to read the account of the wilderness wandering with new literary eyes. As the newly liberated Israelites call out for water, I imagine the deep trenches in my backyard after months of drought and one-hundred-plus degree days. I think of the way I put out dishes of water for stray cats only to find all the water in them quickly evaporated. I think of day after day with the Texas dust turning my black sandals brown and the way a short walk across blacktop in the middle of the day can feel like an endless quest. My experience in Texas gives me new eyes, and new empathy, for ancient Israel's long years of wandering. I am invited into the text in a new way, a way that wasn't available to me before I knew a Texas summer.

Inerrancy, Infallibility, and the Work of Interpretation

One of the most fascinating aspects of my introduction to the study of the Bible in an academic setting was the realization that the people and places referred to in the older and newer testaments are *actual* places and often *actual* historic people referred to in extrabiblical (i.e., broader historical) sources. This realization may seem obvious, but it hit me like a ton of bricks. I remember going on a class trip to Greece and Turkey and standing on one of the ancient Roman roads on a deserted plain in Turkey. I looked down at the stone and thought, "My shoes could be touching the same place Paul's sandals touched thousands of years ago." It brought Scripture to life in a profound new way.

Back in the classroom, I learned about the many (many!) contested aspects of identifying the factuality of authors, dates, and even places in many parts of Scripture. For example, there is a long and contested debate about when the exodus took place and which pharaoh it involved. The two most common proposals are in either the fifteenth or the thirteenth century BCE. This is a difference of a couple hundred years, so not a big deal except that it sets in motion the dating for all the subsequent events of the wilderness wanderings and conquest narratives of Joshua, plus, if we work backward, it establishes a time frame for Joseph's time in Egypt.

Some of you may be aware of the desire to pinpoint the "specifics" of the Bible; those with this inclination often use the language of "inerrancy." I distinguish the terms "inerrant" and "infallible" this way: inerrancy proclaims that Scripture is without any error, while infallibility proclaims that Scripture contains all things necessary for salvation and won't lead us astray from those necessities. Our current understanding of inerrancy finds its roots in the 1978 Chicago Statement on Biblical Inerrancy (CSBI) and the follow-up 1982 Chicago Statement on Biblical Hermeneutics (CSBH). In these two statements, prominent evangelical biblical scholars and church leaders aimed to respond to a rise in claims of subjective interpretations of Scripture or the appeal to the traditions and creeds of the church rather than what can be found in Scripture alone. We won't get into the details of these two statements (they are easy to track down online), but I do want to highlight the centrality of inerrancy and its consequences. In the CSBI, biblical inerrancy and infallibility are defined in this way:

> Article XI.
>
> We affirm that Scripture, having been given by divine inspiration, is infallible, so that, far from misleading us, it is true and reliable in all the matters it addresses.
>
> We deny that it is possible for the Bible to be at the same time infallible and errant in its assertions. Infallibility and inerrancy may be distinguished, but not separated.
>
> Article XII.
>
> We affirm that Scripture in its entirety is inerrant, being free from all falsehood, fraud, or deceit.
>
> We deny that Biblical infallibility and inerrancy are limited to spiritual, religious, or redemptive themes, exclusive of assertions in the fields of history and science. We further deny that scientific hypotheses about earth history may properly be used to overturn the teaching of Scripture on creation and the flood.[3]

Notice the difference between my definitions and the CSBI definitions, particularly regarding the relationship between inerrancy and infallibility.

3. International Council on Biblical Inerrancy, *Chicago Statement on Biblical Inerrancy*, 5.

For the CSBI, the two are "distinguished, but not separated." In other words, for Scripture to not be misleading (infallible), it must be spiritually, religiously, scientifically, and historically true (inerrant). The examples of the creation account and the flood perfectly capture the CSBI's position. While this statement is older than I am, the sentiment continues into the present moment and can be seen most clearly in certain evangelical universities requiring its professors to sign a statement of belief in young-earth creationism, the historicity of Adam and Eve, and the occurrence of a literal flood in order to teach there.

The subsequent CSBH expands on this understanding of the inerrant and infallible nature of Scripture by clarifying their position in the language of hermeneutical (i.e., interpretive) principles:

> Article VI.
>
> We affirm that the Bible expresses God's truth in propositional statements, and we declare that biblical truth is both objective and absolute. We further affirm that a statement is true if it represents matters as they actually are, but is an error if it misrepresents the facts.
>
> Article VII.
>
> We affirm that the meaning expressed in each biblical text is single, definite and fixed.
>
> We deny that the recognition of this single meaning eliminates the variety of its application.[4]

These articles clarify the earlier statements about the truthfulness of Scripture as being literal, objective, absolute, and singular. For these councils, Scripture being inerrant and infallible means that our job as interpreters is to identify the one literal meaning of any given text. This singular meaning still allows us to apply a passage to our lives in a variety of ways, but that application comes only after we have identified properly what the Bible says on any given matter. And what the Bible says is propositional in nature.[5] The work of interpretation, then, is to find this propositional

4. International Council on Biblical Inerrancy, *Chicago Statement on Biblical Hermeneutics*, 2.

5. By "propositional," I mean that the Bible is understood as consistently making clear-cut judgments or assertions (propositions) that lead to obvious and explicit actions. A fine example of propositional statements can be found in the Ten Commandments ("Thou shall not . . .").

statement within the Bible's narratives, legal and religious materials, poetry, genealogies, wisdom sayings, and so on.

The CSBH goes on to clarify how exactly we should read Scripture:

> Article XV.
>
> We affirm the necessity of interpreting the Bible according to its literal, or normal, sense. The literal sense is the grammatical-historical sense, that is, the meaning which the writer expressed. Interpretation according to the literal sense will take account of all figures of speech and literary forms found in the text.
>
> We deny the legitimacy of any approach to Scripture that attributes to it meaning which the literal sense does not support.[6]

To read the Bible literally means here that you read it in its original historical context, which requires knowledge of biblical languages, historical setting, and, as best as you can access it, authorial intention. This strategy for interpreting Scripture serves as the bedrock for many biblical interpreters to this day, particularly in evangelical circles.

The dangers and challenges of this kind of reading strategy are many. I will not unfold all of those dangers here, but I will point to two key examples that demonstrate my reasons for encouraging us to move in a different direction—a direction that affirms the infallibility of Scripture without the claim of inerrancy. The first challenge is that the Chicago statements place the biblical witness and scientific discovery in opposition to each other. Rather than encouraging us to study God's revelation both in Scripture and in creation as beneficial for theological inquiry, the Chicago statements treat the Bible as a modern "scientific" text employed to do work that it did not set out to do in its historical context.[7] The second challenge is the tremendous responsibility placed on interpreters to get it "right" in order to apply Scripture to their daily lives. There is one singular interpretation of Scripture that offers a clear-cut propositional claim, and the interpreter better be sure to get it right. And if two interpreters disagree, then a lot is at stake. Further, as often happens in biblical studies, archaeological or linguistic discoveries that challenge a previously

6. International Council on Biblical Inerrancy, *Chicago Statement on Biblical Hermeneutics*, 3.

7. If you want a resource where the scientific and religious accounts are not antagonistic to one another and that still takes the theological-biblical account seriously, a great place to start is John Walton's *The Lost World of Genesis One*.

assumed date or location run the risk of completely upending previous understandings of a normative interpretation. This kind of situation is precisely what leads to the two different dates (and possibly more) for the exodus. These challenges lead me to an alternative approach to the one set out by the Chicago statements, an approach that muddies the waters of "objective" interpretation without dissolving into a puddle of subjectivity and relativity. To do this, we will look to the study of hermeneutics.

Reading as an Event: Gadamer's *Truth and Method*

A key figure within hermeneutical theory is Hans-Georg Gadamer. In his seminal work, *Truth and Method*, Gadamer hopes to correct overconfidence in our ability to reason ourselves scientifically to an absolute and objective understanding. He responds in the second edition's foreword to the misunderstanding of his work as a manual for interpretation or some other kind of practical application, clarifying that his concern is "not what we do or what we ought to do, but *what happens to us over and above our wanting and doing*."[8] Gadamer's aim is to speak truthfully about what it is we do when we read—not what we hope to do or even what we delude ourselves into thinking we can accomplish in the act of interpretation. He hopes to describe the very human act of meaning-making, pushing his readers to recognize the unavoidably messy and involved work of interpretation. Gadamer builds on the work of his teacher Martin Heidegger, who describes how we arrive at understanding through a kind of "hermeneutical circle."[9] This circular motion of understanding assumes that we come to a text (or anything we interpret) with a preunderstanding that is revised or corrected through the act of interpretation.

To return to the baking metaphor, I come to a recipe for molasses cookies with certain expectations about the outcome. I have eaten a molasses cookie before, I know (whether I am fully cognizant of it or not) that a molasses cookie should taste, look, and smell a certain way because I have prefigured, if you will, the cookie. This example may feel obtuse, likely because it is incredibly obvious: we come to any kind of making (e.g., making meaning or making cookies) with expectations. Language

8. Gadamer, *Truth and Method*, xxvi (italics original).
9. Gadamer, *Truth and Method*, 269.

works on this same presupposition of understanding; that is, we speak to someone with the anticipation that we will understand what the other person says. Anyone who has learned a new language understands well the importance of those preconceptions and building blocks for reaching any kind of understanding through translation. We employ the knowledge of our first language to serve as the foundation for understanding a new one. I come to a molasses cookie recipe with a preconception, what Gadamer comfortably calls (and we likely uncomfortably call) "prejudice."[10] This prejudgment gives me the ability to navigate a recipe and anticipate the likely outcome, but it can also be corrected. I may be surprised when a molasses cookie recipe calls for black pepper and a dash of apple cider vinegar, but I also come to learn something new when these before-unthought-of additions produce a superior cookie.[11] My preconceptions have been confronted with a new insight that transforms my understanding of what a molasses cookie could and should be. Here we find the hermeneutical circle at work.

In this, the scientific age, Gadamer identifies a loss. This loss is one of recognizing the historical nature of ourselves. We find ourselves placed in a particular place and time with particular, historically realized traditions that give us an interpretive baseline for understanding. An unfortunate outcome of the Enlightenment, Gadamer argues, is this loss of rootedness in historical particularity, which includes the preconceptions that have been given to us, whether we are aware of them or not. We simply cannot escape or reason ourselves out of the fact that we are shaped by the historical situation we find ourselves in. In our attempt to attain mastery over the sciences, including the historical ones, we have forgotten "that history does not belong to us; we belong to it."[12] We are historically embedded creatures.

This reminder that we are historically located, that we come to any task with preconceptions that we may or may not be cognizant of, helps us better understand the work of interpretation. Understanding, Gadamer contends, occurs in this middle position between a historically produced text

10. Gadamer, *Truth and Method*, 273. Gadamer here notes that "the history of ideas shows that not until the Enlightenment does the concept of prejudice acquire the negative connotations familiar today. Actually, 'prejudice' means a judgment that is rendered before all the elements that determine a situation have been finally examined."

11. Shoutout to Claire Saffitz and her brilliant cookbook *Dessert Person*.

12. Gadamer, *Truth and Method*, 278.

and a historically bound reader. Making meaning from a text is much more like entering a conversation than studying an object under a microscope. We are not objective observers in interpretation, but we bring ourselves to the text in much the same way as we bring ourselves to anything else we do. Gadamer speaks of reading in terms of a kind of humility, which is an ability to recognize that we come to a text ready to be corrected by it and to discover something new—what Gadamer speaks of as the fusion of horizons.[13]

Importantly, what we find in the act of reading is an event and an opportunity to be transformed. Gadamer writes, "We have the ability to open ourselves to the superior claim the text makes and to respond to what it has to tell us." Hermeneutics, he continues, "is not 'knowledge as domination'—i.e., an appropriation as taking possession; rather, it consists in subordinating itself to the text's claim to dominate our minds."[14] In reading, we encounter texts that have something to teach us. Being a good reader, then, shares features with being a good conversation partner. We come to the conversation with a sufficient baseline ability to engage in dialogue (say, sharing the same language) but also sufficient humility to learn something new and be transformed through the encounter.

You can see how this relates to the earlier statement on biblical inerrancy and hermeneutics. The CSBH directly addresses some of what Gadamer calls "prejudice" and the statement calls "preunderstanding": "We affirm that any preunderstandings which the interpreter brings to Scripture should be in harmony with scriptural teaching and subject to correction by it. We deny that Scripture should be required to fit alien preunderstandings, inconsistent with itself; such as naturalism, evolutionism, scientism, secular humanism, and relativism" (Article XIX, p. 4). The key difference between Gadamer's conversation and the statement's approach has to do with posture or disposition, which leads to a chicken-or-the-egg debate. How does one harmonize with Scripture teaching without being corrected and taught by the text? How do we know what correction comes from within the text and what comes from our own preunderstandings that then confirm our understanding of the text? How do we know that what we deem to be "alien" to the text isn't actually our preunderstanding of what the text is aiming to accomplish?

13. Gadamer, *Truth and Method*, 305.
14. Gadamer, *Truth and Method*, 310.

Is it possible that the ancient writer of the creation accounts in Genesis 1–3 did not have evolution or the refuting of it in mind but was trying to accomplish a different goal?

Gadamer's approach offers us a more realistic starting place, one where we may be so self-aware as to understand our own *pre*understanding commitments.[15] As a bit of a silly, but helpful, example, consider the language in Scripture of God as "the Lord of hosts." This title for God *could* appear to speak of God's radical hospitality, being the greatest of hosts and welcoming all to the table. But, in fact, the language here is about God as leader of the hosts of armies and as a great warrior. This is a very different angle on what it means for God to be over the hosts. Of course, it is easy to research this designation and clarify the meaning, but many other inferences in Scripture are not so easily uncovered. And many of our own biases are much more inconspicuous, even to ourselves. I worry that if we approach Scripture with too much confidence in our abilities to discern the singular and objective meaning, we may miss the word God has for us completely.

The Invitation: Wolfgang Iser's *The Act of Reading*

This reflection on the place where text and reader meet to form meaning continues in Gadamer's student Wolfgang Iser. In *The Act of Reading*, Iser's main goal is to clarify the reading event as an "aesthetic response."[16] Iser makes use of the language of response to capture the "dialectic relationship between text, reader, and their interaction." In a dialectic relationship, the response, "although it is brought about by the text, . . . brings into play the imaginative and perceptive faculties of the reader, in order to make him adjust and even differentiate his own focus."[17] In this definition, we can see Iser's continuity with Gadamer's philosophical hermeneutics: reading brings together text and reader in ways that produce not only interpretation of the text but transformation of the reader.

15. What I mean here by *pre*understanding commitments are those things that serve as the foundation for how we understand the world. For example, when I am baking and am told to add a teaspoon of baking powder, I *already know* that a teaspoon is less than a tablespoon before I head to my baking drawer. I come to a recipe with some knowledge already baked in.

16. Iser, *Act of Reading*, x.

17. Iser, *Act of Reading*, x.

Importantly, Iser emphasizes the active role of the reader in bringing about meaning from the text. This point may seem readily apparent, except that we often undervalue what we, in our particularity, bring to the text. It is easy to recognize that texts in some way need readers to bear meaning. Sharing a kinship with the adage "If a tree falls in the forest and no one hears, does it make a sound?" is the question we might ask: "Can a text, unread, be the bearer of meaning?" Iser draws out more than the overt claim that a text needs readers to bear meaning; he argues that a reader's particular historical location plays an *active* role in meaning-making. This active role means that the text can come to mean different things not only for different readers but even for the same reader who arrives at different meaning at different times.[18]

Iser's contention is not an anything-goes approach where interpreting texts means that any text can mean anything. Remember, meaning arises as an event where reader and text meet, which means the text also has something essential to contribute. Instead, Iser focuses on the active role of reader and emphasizes the dynamism of the reading event, where reading is itself a kind of "entanglement."[19] This entanglement with the text engrosses our attention:

> While we are caught up in a text, we do not at first know what is happening to us. This is why we often feel the need to talk about books we have read—not in order to gain some distance from them so much as to find out just what it is we were entangled in. . . . When we are present in an event, something must happen to us. The more "present" the text is to us, the more our habitual selves—at least for the duration of the reading—recede into the "past."[20]

Iser's description of the reading event captures the experience I imagine many of us have had where we find ourselves unable to put a book down, so caught up in the narrative world that for a moment (or maybe hours) we do not need to "suspend belief" to reside in a storied world. We are there, in some paradoxical way.

J. R. R. Tolkien, in his remarkable essay "On Fairy-Stories," similarly captures this idea of readerly entanglement, in the context of reading the

18. Iser, *Act of Reading*, 97.
19. Iser, *Act of Reading*, 131.
20. Iser, *Act of Reading*, 131.

mythical and fantastic. He notes that the moment readers feel they must suspend disbelief, the enchantment of dwelling within a storied world is removed and readers are left "looking at the little abortive Secondary World from the outside."[21] That is, readers do not suspend disbelief in reading fairy-stories; instead, they dwell within and believe the truth of the stories as they engage the fictional world. Tolkien recognizes that children are much better at indwelling these fantastical worlds by making the fictional world *true* and not make-believe.[22] Adults, on the other hand, struggle to permit themselves this enchantment, much like a second-rate sports fan watching a game while staving off boredom.[23] The childlike posture Tolkien hopes to cultivate in his audience parallels Iser's philosophical claim that a genuine reading event involves becoming entangled with the story, rather than seeking to extract meaning from it like an archaeologist out on a dig.[24] The reading event is not about domination of the text but about the possibility of transformed readers.

Iser expands on the idea of readerly entanglement by speaking of readers as taking on a "wandering viewpoint."[25] The text, Iser observes, cannot be consumed by the reader all at once in the way we might take in a work of fine art or sculpture. We must travel *through* the text in order to arrive at an understanding of it. While there are many similarities between viewing a work of art and reading a text—what Gadamer refers to as a kind of "play" in *Truth and Method*—there are also obvious differences.

As a teenager and into my early adulthood, I used to make regular visits to a particular painting of Salvador Dalí at the free art museum in my hometown. I would first stand back and take in the whole scene before stepping closer to examine the mix of highly realistic and utterly abstract images painted across the canvas. Every time I visited this painting, I would

21. Tolkien, "On Fairy-Stories," 60.

22. Tolkien, "On Fairy-Stories," 60–61.

23. Tolkien, "On Fairy-Stories," 61.

24. Iser, *Act of Reading*, 5. Iser pointedly goes after this excavational and erroneous posture of reading when he writes, "If this meaning, as the very heart of the work, can be lifted out of the text, the work is then used up—through interpretation, literature is turned into an item for consumption" (5). Gadamer similarly critiques this kind of posture in broader terms: "The whole value of hermeneutical experience—like knowledge in general—seemed to consist in the fact that here we are not simply filing things in pigeonholes but that what we encounter in tradition says something to us. Understanding, then, does not consist in technical virtuosity of 'understanding' everything written. Rather, it is a genuine experience (*Erfahrung*)—i.e., an encounter with something that asserts itself as truth." Gadamer, *Truth and Method*, 483.

25. Iser, *Act of Reading*, 108–18.

see something new, depending both on my mood and on what caught my eye on that viewing. But the way I read and return to literature is different. I have read *The Lord of the Rings* more than any other work of literature. On each reread, I open the first chapter to read: "When Mr. Bilbo Baggins of Bag End announced that he would shortly be celebrating his eleventy-first birthday . . ."[26] I cannot step back and take the whole sweep of the story in a glance as I can with the Dalí painting. While in both the painting and the novel I can find something new on each viewing or reading, I find meaning in a text differently than in an image. Iser captures this distinctiveness by noting, "The fact [is] that the whole text can never be perceived at any one time. In this respect it differs from given objects, which can generally be viewed or at least conceived as a whole."[27] When reading literature, we must build the narrative world as the story unfolds, and that world building requires us as readers to produce all the raw imaginative material to image that world.

As we read, we adopt a wandering viewpoint where our expectations are met or thwarted. (Say that we first imagine Bilbo, at nearly 111, to appear quite old, until we are told a few lines later that he looks half his age.) As we read the story, we are continually taking in new information and refiguring the world we have built. Iser describes this as an "intersection between retention and pretension," where each new line of a story expands, modifies, or adapts our understanding of the story as a whole.[28] Here, we can see the active role of the reader at work within Iser's understanding of the reading event.

For me, one of the most profound stories in the Pentateuch is that of Genesis 32, where Jacob wrestles with a mysterious man all night. We will explore this story in more detail in chapter 3, but for now I want us to simply consider how we heard this story when it was read to us for the first, second, and third times. The first time the story was read or introduced to us, probably via a children's Bible, we may have focused on certain parts—likely the gifting of the blessing and new name near the end of the story. The second time we read it, we may have paused to consider how Jacob

26. Tolkien, *Lord of the Rings*, 21.

27. Iser, *Act of Reading*, 108–9. In a later interview, Iser draws out the distinction between texts and objects, noting that, while perception plays a role when one is viewing an object, "when one reads a text, there are no given objects to be perceived; instead objects must be built up from the knowledge invoked or the information provided." Iser, Holland, and Booth, "Interview," 63.

28. Iser, *Act of Reading*, 111.

was feeling during this all-night wrestling match: Did he get tired? (I know I would!) Was he scared? (I would be, if I were wrestling with someone I couldn't see in the pitch black of night.) How violent was this wrestling match? Was there bruising, blood, a need for stitches? The third time we read it, we may have come across the story as we were reading through the larger Jacob story. We may have known that he travels toward his estranged brother, who has every reason to kill him. We may have thought about our own feelings about estranged family members or times we were caught off-guard and our life radically changed in a moment. All this to say, we provide the imaginative fuel that carries the story forward and makes it meaningful as we wander through a text. We are entangled in the meaning that we make, and for that reason we ourselves are transformed as we read. Meaning resides not somewhere "out there" but within us. Akin to taking a trip to a new place, through encountering a text, we learn new things about ourselves. And with each reread we find that there is more to be discovered in both the text and ourselves.

Where Hermeneutics Meets Biblical Study

The hermeneutical claim that reading is an event—one that invites us as readers into an encounter and puts us at risk of correction and transformation—finds fertile soil in biblical studies. Gadamer's critique of the Enlightenment as denying the fact that all readers come to texts subjectively—that is, with preconceptions that guide our expectations in reading—focuses in particular on the historical sciences, which include and in many ways are exemplified in the historical-critical method of reading Scripture. Gadamer highlights that by insisting that the Bible be approached as a historical document stripped of creedal bias, Enlightened readers do not free themselves of the prejudice they seek to avoid for the sake of objectivity but rather show their own "prejudice against prejudice."[29] That is, critical readers of Scripture, in trying to cast off all the dogmatic claims of the text and draw out the truth untethered from the subjective claims, do not remove the historically conditioned preconceptions—those that Gadamer insists are necessary for any kind of understanding—so much as replace one preconception (say, that Scripture

29. Gadamer, *Truth and Method*, 273.

is authoritative and God-breathed) with another (say, that "we can know better"[30]).

This desire to remove all subjectivity in order to become objective observers of historical texts in the same manner as we observe the natural world distorts not only the text we read but who we understand ourselves to be. Gadamer asks, "Does being situated within traditions really mean being subject to prejudices and limited in one's freedom? Is not, rather, all human existence, even the freest, limited and qualified in various ways?"[31] Gadamer insists that "reason exists for us only in concrete, historical terms—i.e., it is not its own master but remains constantly dependent on the given circumstances in which it operates."[32] In making "unbiased" reason the adjudicator of truthfulness, we lose sight not only of what the text might have to say to us but of who we are.

In his *Theology of the Old Testament*, Walter Brueggemann makes a similar observation as he outlines the rise of the historical-critical method and its consequences for biblical interpretation.[33] When scholars treat the Bible like any other book through the use of historical-critical tools, "the Bible itself became the material that was assessed and measured, and in some cases found wanting."[34] And with the biblical scholar dissecting the scriptural texts with the same objective posture as the natural scientist, this critical methodology supported "the new importance of the individual scholar and the scholarly guild," making the "biblical text subservient, at least methodologically, to the rational claims of the interpretive elite."[35]

Brueggemann, in the same spirit as Gadamer, laments the consequences of the critical dissection of the Bible not simply as a misunderstanding of the text but as a false view of the interpreter as an "unencumbered objective interpreter who was understood to be a nonpartisan, uninvolved reader of the data."[36] This understanding of the objective interpreter made possible a more sinister dynamic, wherein the historical-critical enterprise "cannot tolerate intellectual or theological claims and affirmations that run

30. Gadamer, *Truth and Method*, 274.
31. Gadamer, *Truth and Method*, 277.
32. Gadamer, *Truth and Method*, 277.
33. Brueggemann, *Theology of the Old Testament*, 6–15.
34. Brueggemann, *Theology of the Old Testament*, 10.
35. Brueggemann, *Theology of the Old Testament*, 10.
36. Brueggemann, *Theology of the Old Testament*, 13 (italics that appear in the original have been removed).

against its thin objectivism, which is itself an unacknowledged intellectual, theological claim."[37] Brueggemann here points to the prejudice against prejudice, which is a veiled dogmatic claim that creates an environment where the Old Testament in particular loses its theological authority, especially over the Protestant church (in which the historical-critical method thrived), and is finally "lost in the practice of reductionist criticism."[38] To be clear, while Brueggemann's concern here is related specifically to the Old Testament, the New Testament also finds itself reduced through these critical tools, with the demythologizing of the Gospels and quest for the historical Jesus being two examples of the result.

For Brueggemann, the corrective to this displacement of the Old Testament is found in developing a robust Old Testament theology that returns the text to communities of faith as something beneficial and useful, in a similar spirit to Origen's back in the third century. Many others have recognized the need to respond proactively to the relegation of Scripture, particularly of the Old Testament, to historical dissection.[39] In this book, I will follow those who have taken the literary path to recovering the Old Testament as something of value, beyond merely a historical document for investigation, through the call to view the Bible as literature.

Biblical Poetics

The study of biblical poetics, the theory of literary devices in biblical narrative and poetry, finds its origins in Aristotle's *Poetics*. Aristotle's opening remarks help delineate the study of poetics at large: "Our topic is poetry in itself and its kind, and what potential each has; how plots should be constructed if the composition is to turn out well; also from how many parts it is [constituted], and of what sort they are; and likewise all other aspects of the same enquiry."[40] Notice here that Aristotle speaks of poems as possessing plots, a feature we are more likely to identify with narrative than with poetry. For the ancient Greeks, as for many other ancient

37. Brueggemann, *Theology of the Old Testament*, 14.

38. Brueggemann, *Theology of the Old Testament*, 14.

39. There are too many resources to list all of them here, but these are some good places to begin: Childs, *Introduction to the Old Testament*; Davis, *Getting Involved with God*; Gignilliat, *Reading Scripture Canonically*; Legaspi, *Death of Scripture*; Louth, *Discerning the Mystery*; Vanhoozer, *Is There a Meaning in This Text?*; Westphal, *Whose Community?*

40. Aristotle, *Poetics* 47a8–15, para. 1.

civilizations (including ancient Israel), the clear distinction between poetry and narrative would be unfamiliar. For Aristotle and his Greek audience in particular, the great stories of the gods and epic heroes are found in long and winding poetic tales, maybe most familiar to us through Homer's *Iliad* and *Odyssey*. In fact, poetic verse was so prevalent in Aristotle's context that he must clarify that his exploration of poetry in this work is about the artistry of representation, not ascribing the poetic "indiscriminately, according to [a work's use] of verse."[41] Aristotle here introduces the need for an expansive discourse on poetics because he has found no designated and focused study of the form particular to literary representation. His study meets this need through an exploration of poetics centering on literary form and extrapolated through the study of great texts.

I begin my discussion of biblical poetics with Aristotle because it is important to be clear that poetics has to do with the artistry of storytelling and not simply our more narrowly defined contemporary conceptions of poetry. This distinction aids us not only in understanding the term "poetics" but also in recognizing the literary quality particular to biblical Hebrew narrative. While we have standout examples of poetic verse (in songs like those of Miriam and Hannah or in the Psalter), the categories of "poetry" and "narrative" would be foreign to ancient writers and readers. We can deduce certain poetic devices (like parallelism) common in the Old Testament, but the clear division between types of artistry simply does not exist in biblical Hebrew narrative.[42] In the most general terms (and recognizing the variability within the text itself), biblical poetics can be understood as distinguishing biblical narrative from biblical poetry with the use of a general sentence structure in narrative portions (called variously the *waw*-consecutive, the *wayyiqtol*, or the consecutive-preterite) and the use of parallelism in poetry.[43]

41. Aristotle, *Poetics* 47b10–20, para. 2.

42. Robert Alter captures this lack of clear delineation between poetry and narrative when he notes, "Because the poems are not set out as poetry in the traditional Hebrew text, there are sometimes serious questions as to where the line breaks should come and, especially in some of the Prophets, ambiguities about the boundaries between prose and poetic passages." Alter, *Art of Biblical Poetry*, 5.

43. Robert Lowth's *De Sacra Poesi Hebræorum* (1753) serves as the seminal work on biblical poetry, which has been built on and refined since. Two more contemporary and helpful resources on biblical poetry's use of parallelism are found in Robert Alter's *The Art of Biblical Poetry* and J. P. Fokkelman's *Reading Biblical Poetry*. The ongoing work of drawing out the distinctive qualities of Hebrew poetry without overstating the case can be seen in the work of Rebecca Poe

I will make use of important contributions from the field of biblical poetics and from the broader study of literary theory to demonstrate the invitation to readers found through the narratives in Scripture's first five books. Robert Alter's *The Art of Biblical Narrative* (1981), arguably the most influential of these contributions, introduced generations of scholars and students to the importance of viewing the Hebrew Bible as literature. Alter's training in English and comparative literature enabled him to see biblical Hebrew narrative with fresh eyes for the religious studies guild. He comments in his preface that a rather casual presentation on the literary qualities of Genesis 38–39 a decade before the book's publication "turned out to be rather more successful than the carefully meditated public lectures on modern Jewish writing" that he was giving that same week.[44]

Stumbling into this literary study of biblical narrative, Alter found a receptive audience who recognized the value of his contribution to broader scholarship. One reviewer wrote that in combining training in literary theory with a clear command of the Hebrew language, Alter offers a work that "is not only refreshing, but even vital to all Bible-readers who, conditioned by the rigors of 'excavative scholarship,' are still of the opinion that the Bible-as-literature is merely one facet or a diminishing experience rather than a decisive judgment."[45] This early review foreshadowed the impact this work would have in the subsequent decades, not only in the lofty realm of academic study, but in the lives of Jewish and Christian faith communities.

In *The Art of Biblical Narrative*, Alter centrally argues that the artistry of Hebrew narrative elucidates theological meaning. Alter identifies the challenge to modern readers (even literary, astute ones) in recognizing ancient biblical Hebrew narratives' distinctive literary features as more than "crude," "simple," or "primitive": "What we need to understand better is that the religious vision of the Bible is given depth and subtlety precisely by being conveyed through the most sophisticated resources of prose fiction."[46] That is, we must not sell these ancient storytellers short in

Hays, *The Function of Story in the Hebrew Psalter*, wherein she argues that narrative elements appear in the poetry of the Psalms.

44. Alter, *Art of Biblical Narrative*, xv.

45. Fokkelman, review of *The Art of Biblical Narrative*, 441.

46. Alter, *Art of Biblical Narrative*, 23.

their ability to speak richly about the human encounter with God. While the literary approach differs from many of those that are normative today, the distinctive artistry of biblical Hebrew narrative should not be underappreciated. As Alter summarizes, "Almost the whole range of biblical narrative . . . embodies the basic perception that man must live before God, in the transforming medium of time, incessantly and perplexingly in relation with others; and a literary perspective on the operations of narrative may help us more than any other to see how this perception was translated into stories that have had such a powerful, enduring hold on the imagination."[47]

Attending to the artistry of biblical narrative helps us acutely recognize the confounding claim that God communes with the creatures God has made. My invitation to readers of the Pentateuch builds on Alter's insistence that the artistry of biblical Hebrew narrative is central for conveying meaning. I will make use of not only Alter's insights on biblical narrative throughout this work but also occasionally his work in Bible translations to draw out the artistry of the text, as bearer of theological meaning.[48]

We need to recognize the ways that theology is interwoven into the artistry of biblical narrative. Reading biblical narrative is more demanding than stripping stories of their artistry to get at the moral, but it is also more rewarding. The result of holding the theological and artistic together invites us as readers into a transformative reading event. We are invited into an experience, not simply to receive a lesson in morality or archaeology. As best as we can tell, the biblical authors and editors understood themselves as telling stories of the God of Israel. We lose out on so much of the richness and reward of reading these stories when we strip them of their narrative artistry.

One of the greatest challenges to recognizing the artistry of biblical narratives results from reading the text in translation. Hebrew's bare-bones narrative style is often glossed over when rendered into our English vernacular in our desire for readable and accessible stories. These translations offer the more reader-friendly narrative cues that English speakers expect but leave readers with less of the narrative artistry by filling in the gaps and smoothing out the stops and starts that characterize biblical Hebrew narrative. Consequently, the curt, spare quality of Hebrew narrative is frequently overlooked in interpretation.

47. Alter, *Art of Biblical Narrative*, 24.
48. Alter, *Hebrew Bible*, vol. 1.

This interpretive challenge centers on two concerns. First, when we lose sight of the bare-bones quality of biblical Hebrew narrative, the invitation to readerly wonder gets skewed—even lost. Stories that feature starts and stops, strange syntax, and brief and disjunctive descriptions of climactic events might be more challenging for us to read, but perhaps ambiguity and opportunity, rather than smoothness and clarity, should guide readers' encounters with the text. Second, in losing sight of the spare quality of the Pentateuch, we also lose the artistry of this ancient form of storytelling. In a more recent work, *The Art of Bible Translation* (2019), Alter once again emphasizes the artistry of the biblical writers and the importance of the translator's attunement to this artistry: "The Hebrew Bible by and large exhibits consummate artistry in the language of its narratives and of its poetry, and there must be an answering art in the translation in order to convey what is remarkable about the original."[49] Alter argues that in trying to make contemporary biblical translations more "accessible," we have also made the translations "stylistically inferior in nearly all respects."[50] For Alter, the most *recent* translation that reflects some of the spirit of biblical narrative can be found in the King James Version (1611), which is "by no means the same as reading it in Hebrew," yet "much from the themes and imagery and characterization of the Hebrew is nevertheless preserved."[51]

I am not raising the issue of translation to dissuade anyone from using a post-seventeenth-century translation. Instead, I believe that the recognition that something is lost in translation and an awareness of some of those stylistic features not readily apparent in, say, the NRSV, NIV, or ESV can enrich our reading of the text in translation and invite us more deeply into these biblical stories. And, for those who are currently learning biblical Hebrew or who hope to learn it someday, an awareness of the artistry may make the process of verb conjugation and the frequent sometimes-but-not-always rules of the language more enjoyable by seeing the text not only as a syntactical challenge but as an artistic invitation.

49. Alter, *Art of Bible Translation*, 16.
50. Alter, *Pen of Iron*, 9–10.
51. Alter, *Pen of Iron*, 26.

CHAPTER 2

Brevity

Introduction

I love reading long and winding tales of epic quests and fantastic worlds. Many of my favorite "fun reading" books are written as part of trilogies or extended series. I enjoy the ease of entering into a story rich with world-building description and detailed dialogues that reveal complex and dynamic relationships. If it hasn't been made clear by now, *The Lord of the Rings* serves as the exemplar of grand storytelling for me, with its impressive scope and well-rounded characters. The story contains offshoots and allusions to other stories within the world of Middle Earth. Some of these allusions will be familiar to those who have read *The Hobbit*, while other, more obscure references require familiarity with *The Silmarillion*, *The Unfinished Tales*, and the histories of Middle Earth. *The Lord of the Rings* offers an abundance of detail, background, even invented languages to keep a reader busy through many, many reads. A very different mode of modern storytelling—though no less creative or profound—can be found in the short-story form. Unlike the novel, these brief works of prose unfold their tales with fewer narrative cues and often a smaller cast of characters. The story must be told more sparely in this confined space.[1]

A parallel to the distinction between the modern novel and the short story can be found, though maybe not perfectly, in the difference between

1. My book *Flannery O'Connor and Stylistic Asceticism* explores the theological impact of spare narration in both biblical Hebrew narrative and Flannery O'Connor's fiction.

watching a television series and watching a movie. After a long day, I find that I prefer watching an episode from a television show because it doesn't require the same level of focused attention as a movie. Because the show has an entire season's worth of episodes to unfold its story, every minute counts for less, if you will, than it does in a movie that only has two hours to tell its tale. Similarly, each line of a novel contributes less to the narrative arc than the individual lines of a short story. The difference here is simply about quantity, not quality. We can likely think of many a brilliant television show that outdoes the artistry of a subpar film, and vice versa.

I raise the differences between the modern novel and the short story and between a movie and a television series simply because I want us to observe that many of the stories we are accustomed to reading come in a long form, with narrative worlds that capture our attention for over one hundred pages. Even the short stories you might read are likely at least ten to twenty pages long, rather than only a handful of sentences. The kinds of stories we are focusing on in this book are shorter, sometimes much shorter, than those to which we are accustomed.

Because we will be speaking about very short stories that are sometimes only a few lines long, let me define what I mean by "story" in biblical Hebrew narrative. We find in the Old Testament a collection of stories, sometimes referred to as "cycles," centered on one figure. For example, Genesis 5:28–9:29 focuses on Noah. A series of events occurs:

- Noah is born, lives five hundred years, and fathers three sons (Gen. 5:28–32).
- God looks at the disordered world, including the pairing of humans with the Nephilim, and finds only wickedness, except for in the figure of Noah (6:1–9).
- God instructs Noah to build an ark in preparation for a great flood (6:11–22).
- Noah and his human and animal companions find safety on the ark as rain falls for forty days and nights and a great flood wipes out everything on the earth (7:1–24).
- After 150 days, the waters subside, and Noah sends out a dove to confirm that the land is once again dry (8:1–12).

- Noah sees that the ground is dry and leaves the ark along with all his companions, as God had instructed him to do (8:13–19).
- God makes a promise to Noah and his descendants, which God confirms by establishing a covenant with Noah and his sons (8:20–9:17).
- Noah plants a vineyard, becomes drunk, and lies uncovered in his tent. We are told that one son "saw his nakedness," but the other two covered his nakedness with faces turned away (9:18–27).
- A brief narrative summary notes that Noah lives for another 350 years after the flood, dying at the age of 950 (Gen. 9:28–29).

All these events could be said to be the story of Noah. But this larger story contains within it stand-alone stories. Some of these stand-alone stories can be broken down into even smaller stories, like Genesis 8:20–9:17, where we find three mini-stories: God's promise to Noah (8:20–22), God's blessing of Noah and his sons (9:1–7), and God establishing a covenant with them (9:8–17). Within the story of Noah is the story of God committing himself to Noah and his descendants, and within this smaller story are three stories about promise, blessing, and covenant. I realize that this explanation likely doesn't help in clearly delineating what makes a story a story, but I do think it is important to note that stories can function, especially in biblical Hebrew narrative, like Russian nesting dolls, with a story appearing within a story and so on.

I will be working with a "bare minimum" definition of a story—one that precludes certain things, like the narrative summary that closes out the Noah cycle, from being considered a story. Rebecca Poe Hays, in *The Function of Story in the Hebrew Psalter*, argues that too sharp a delineation between poetry and narrative in the Psalms overlooks the presence of story within its poetic form. In order to demonstrate the presence of story in the Psalms, Hays must first define "story." Her definition of a story offers a solid framework to identify story not only in the Psalms but more broadly in biblical Hebrew narrative, where stories are sometimes quite spare but are still very much stories. Hays defines three related terms: "moments," "portraits," and "stories." A "moment" is the "most basic building block" in a story, and she defines it as "a description of a single action or state in a clause governed by one active or passive verb."[2] A

2. Hays, *Function of Story*, 17.

"portrait" is "some arrangement of moments" that are not yet narrative but are more extended descriptions than moments.[3] Moments chained together "in clear sequential and/or casual relationships" produce stories. So the distinction for Hays between non-narrative portraits and narrative stories has to do with the relationship a cluster of moments have to one another: Is there a chronological or effectual relationship between these moments? If yes, this is a story; if no, this is a portrait.

To more clearly draw out these distinctions and to establish how I will define "story," consider these two accounts from the Noah cycle of moments, portraits, and stories.

> Noah was a righteous man [moment 1], blameless in his generation [moment 2]; Noah walked with God [moment 3]. And Noah had three sons, Shem, Ham, Japheth [moment 4]. (Gen. 6:9–10 NRSV)

> Then the LORD said to Noah, "Go into the ark . . . [moment 1]. For in seven days I will send rain . . ." [moment 2]. And Noah did all that the LORD had commanded him [moment 3]. (Gen. 7:1–5 NRSV)

Genesis 6:9–10 is an example of a portrait. Notice that the moments in these verses do not have a chronological or causal connection to each other. We gain a portrait of Noah here, but we don't see the unfolding of a story. Whereas in Genesis 7:1–5, which is a story, we see a chronological linking of events: God tells Moses to build an ark *because* in a week God is sending rain. *In response* Noah does all that is asked of him.

It is important to note that my example of a story gets into the sticky bits of how story is generally defined. Hays notes that "stories typically require a minimum of three moments to allow the plot to develop," and she points to Aristotle's definition of beginning, middle, and end.[4] In the account of God's instructions to Noah in Genesis 7:1–5, we do have a beginning, middle, and end. But two of these three moments occur within God's instructions to Moses. I use this especially brief example to demonstrate how stories work in biblical Hebrew narrative. They are brief—sometimes so brief that they toe the line between a clear-cut definition of a portrait and a story. What is important, I think, is to recognize two

3. Hays, *Function of Story*, 17.
4. Hays, *Function of Story*, 21.

things. First, stories can be very brief. We recognize them because they string together moments so as to unfold a sequence of events (i.e., they have a beginning, middle, and end). Second, stories exist within stories, and within biblical narrative they can be explored in their most spare forms (e.g., the smallest nesting doll) or in something more substantive, like the Noah cycle.

The Brevity of Biblical Hebrew Narrative

One of the most well-known stories of biblical Hebrew narrative can be found in the story of the binding of Isaac in Genesis 22:1–19. In this compact story, Abraham is told to bring his son Isaac—the same son whose predicted birth made his aged mother, Sarah, laugh at the possibility that she could bear a child—to the place God will show Abraham and to offer his son as a burnt offering to God. This story sticks out for the preposterous command God gives Abraham and for the father's complete obedience in preparing his son as a sacrifice, paired with the lack of any explanation of *why* God asks for this offering, *how* Abraham feels about this request, and *if* Isaac has any inkling of what is happening (the text gives us no indication that he is clued in until they are far along on their journey). We as readers are left with a lot of questions as we try to color in the lines of this sparsely rendered story.

In *Mimesis: The Representation of Reality in Western Literature*, Erich Auerbach begins by comparing the lavish Homeric epic to its stark ancient counterpart in biblical Hebrew narrative.[5] Auerbach looks to Abraham's binding of Isaac in Genesis 22 as the exemplar of biblical narrative, drawing out how an "epic style" equal to Homer's comes by way of "a different world of forms."[6] Auerbach distinguishes between the character of the two epics primarily through contrasting what appears in the foreground and background of the story. Looking to Genesis 22, Auerbach notes, "If we conceive of Abraham in the foreground, where it might be possible to picture him as prostrate or kneeling or bowing with outspread arms or gazing upward, God is not there too: Abraham's words and gestures are directed toward the depths of the picture or upward, but in any case

5. Auerbach, *Mimesis*, 3–23.
6. Auerbach, *Mimesis*, 8.

the undetermined, dark place from which the voice comes to him is not in the foreground."[7]

We have two central characters in this story: God and Abraham (Isaac and Sarah are notably silent). Only one of the characters stands before us as readers. God resides somewhere in the dim background, maybe even offstage, an ominous and disembodied figure bearing down on the scene. Auerbach's observation helps us draw out Alter's point, which we discussed in chapter 1, about the theological motivation for the spare style of biblical narrative. In biblical Hebrew narrative generally, and the Pentateuch in particular, we find a particular narrative form. This spare form was deemed suitable for ancient storytellers to speak about God in relationship with humanity in a way that did not diminish the dissimilarity between a God who is over the cosmos and finite humans who are limited in space and time.

This central claim, that the spare style of biblical Hebrew narrative reflects a theological conviction about God in relationship with humanity, is drawn out in Meir Sternberg's *The Poetics of Biblical Narrative: Ideological Literature and the Drama of Reading*. Sternberg argues that we ought to hold together the conviction that biblical narrative is both a religious text and artistic expression.[8] His assertion that biblical narrative is both pays off as he pushes against the assumption that biblical stories are purely didactic—that they serve to convey a moral or an ethic as their principal aim. In insisting that these stories are didactic, we ask the artistry to take a back seat to uncovering the moral "takeaway." The artistry becomes relegated in favor of the moral of the story, much in the same way as the historical critic ignores the features of storytelling in trying to uncover what really happened, or in the same way the Chicago Statements on inerrancy and hermeneutics insist that the Bible is full of propositional statements. Stories cannot be propositions.

I would guess that many of us have experienced a similar flattening of biblical stories by way of children's Bibles that resolve any inherent tension, like the known world being wiped out in the account of Noah's ark or the enslaved woman Hagar being impregnated and then cast off by Abraham before the miraculous pregnancy of Sarah. Taken from a children's Bible that does a very good job with telling the biblical story simply but truly, here is the story of Noah's ark:

7. Auerbach, *Mimesis*, 9.

8. Sternberg, *Poetics of Biblical Narrative*, 35.

> Before long, people started fighting and hurting one another terribly. God wept that they were not enjoying the lovely earth he had made. Finally, he said, "I must make a new beginning. I will send a flood to cover the whole earth."
>
> But one man named Noah was kind and did what was right.
>
> God told Noah to build a big boat called an ark. Then God said, "Gather all your family and two of every kind of animal, bird, and insect." God sent the rain, and Noah led everyone into the ark. For forty days and forty nights it rained so hard that the water covered even the highest mountains.
>
> Boy, did it smell inside the ark! And the noise! The *ROARing* and *BAAing*, the *NEIGHing* and the *MOOing*! But—amazingly—everyone got along. Yes, even the lion lay down with the lamb.
>
> At last the rain stopped. Noah sent out a dove in search of land. When the bird returned with an olive leaf, Noah and his family cheered. Noah thanked God for saving them.
>
> God told Noah, "I promise not to send another flood to cover the whole earth." And God made a beautiful rainbow so people would never forget his promise.
>
> **Dear God, thank you for rainbows and for keeping your promise to us.**[9]

The retelling of the story of the flood is entirely appropriate for its target audience of readers ages four to eight. It captures the reasons for the flood, Noah's good character, and the tremendous company kept on the ark. While this is a great introduction of the story to children, what we find in Genesis 7 offers us more as mature readers. There we find not only the elements of the story above but the profound death that surrounded the ark in the days of the flood. This is a story of both promise and annihilation, mercy and judgment. To reduce it to simply propositional statements or to a story developmentally appropriate for children feels much like reducing a great work of Rembrandt to a poorly photocopied image. Viewing biblical stories as art invites us into wonder, curiosity, and discovery; these are stories, not propositions. Sternberg notes that "if biblical narrative is didactic, then it has chosen the strangest way to go about its business. . . . Instead of polarizing the reader's emotional and ethical response in line with some preconceived scheme of values, the Bible habitually generates ambivalence."[10] Didactic priorities tempt us to turn rich stories into pithy (and often problematic) instruction manuals for living.

9. Tutu, *Children of God Storybook Bible*, 16–17.
10. Sternberg, *Poetics of Biblical Narrative*, 37–38.

The brief character of biblical Hebrew narrative possesses theological underpinnings. There is a reason for the radical foregrounding of a story like Abraham's binding of Isaac with a key player present only in voice. This spare quality could be understood as primitive storytelling or as simply a didactic tool for getting a point across, but this kind of understanding ignores the theological dimension of Hebrew narrative's artistically economic style. Sternberg notes that in "passing off its art for artlessness," biblical narrative offers us an "unadorned parataxis."[11] "Parataxis" describes how biblical stories unfold succinctly without many subordinate clauses offering us a character's internal thoughts, evocative descriptions of the landscape and setting for the story, or even clues about a character's external appearance.

The brief nature of these stories offers an invitation to explore the depths of meaning within such seemingly simple storylines. And this hidden depth found through challenging readings, Sternberg argues, should be rather unsurprising since these are stories about God and humans: "With the narrative become an obstacle course, its reading turns into a drama of understanding—conflict between inferences, seesawing, reversal, discovery, and all. The only knowledge perfectly acquired is the knowledge of our limitations. It is by a sustained effort alone that the reader can attain at the end to something of the vision that God has possessed all along: to make sense of the discourse is to gain a sense of being human."[12] Sternberg captures the theological import *and* impact of biblical stories.

These stories speak of the God who is over all the cosmos entering into relationship with altogether human figures like Adam, Eve, Noah, Abraham, Sarah, Hagar, Isaac, Rebekah, Jacob, Rachel, and others. Telling these kinds of stories requires that the narrators not overstep or say too much about the God who enters into human affairs. The ambiguity and lack of detailed description amount to a theological recognition that we are speaking about the God of the universe.[13] Here, we see the theological import of the bare-bones style of narration. At the same time, though, the stories also invite readers into this confounding task of discerning God at

11. Sternberg, *Poetics of Biblical Narrative*, 53.

12. Sternberg, *Poetics of Biblical Narrative*, 47.

13. Later, in chapter 4, I explore how when the stories do speak about the character of God, they often do so by using poetic or paradigmatic features so as not to say too much or speak too clearly about this God who is over all creation.

work in the world through wrestling with the text. We discover not only how God is at work in the lives of the ancients but how God remains at work in the world—mysteriously yet truly. The spare style impacts us as readers. Often, it humbles us. I would guess that the shortcut to a more didactic treatment of biblical stories may sometimes be motivated inadvertently by the fact that sitting in this tension and recognizing our own limits is an uncomfortable challenge.

Ancient Near East Parallels and Ancient Israel's Distinctiveness

The artistry we find in biblical Hebrew narrative mirrors in some ways the broader ancient Near East tradition of storytelling. In ancient texts like the Babylonian creation myth, *Enuma Elish*, and the Sumerian poems of *The Epic of Gilgamesh*, we find grand epics that mirror imagery and themes in the biblical creation stories. What is unique to biblical storytelling, though, is that distinctive literary voice in which the stories are told—and notably, their brevity. As we accept the invitation of the stories of the Pentateuch, it is good to recognize both their similarities to and their differences from the broader ancient Near East tradition.

Telling stories concerning god(s) and humanity is not unique to biblical literature. In the form of myths, epics, royal records, letters, chronicles, and songs, such stories are told throughout the ancient Near East.[14] In many ways, the use of comparative methods to bring ancient Israel's text into conversation with the texts produced by Israel's neighbors helps us situate the biblical text in its broader ancient context and, in turn, offers a corrective to reading modern assumptions or priorities too quickly into the text. A prime example of the effectiveness of this approach can be found in John Walton's *The Lost World of Genesis One: Ancient Cosmology and the Origins Debate*. In this work, Walton shows how our modern assumptions that the creation narrative inherently prioritizes physical creation stand in contrast to the assumptions of the ancient world, where accounts of creation have to do with matters of function and purpose rather than materiality. His work offers a way to speak about the truthfulness of the biblical creation account without confusing an ancient story with a modern scientific approach.

14. Two accessible and helpful resources are John H. Walton's *Ancient Near Eastern Thought* and Michael D. Coogan's *A Reader of Ancient Near Eastern Texts*.

Walton's book gives us an approachable way to see how using comparative methods can help us see the biblical text through an ancient lens while allowing it to retain its unique witness. As is often the case, though, sometimes the helpful tools of comparative methodology risk losing sight of the distinctiveness of the biblical account. A few years after Frank Moore Cross's influential *Canaanite Myth and Hebrew Epic: Essays in the History of the Religion of Israel* was published, Shemaryahu Talmon warned against making comparative work too central to interpretation in biblical studies.[15] Talmon insists that when scholars face unclear words, phrases, or ideas, the work of intertextual comparison must take priority over the extratextual. That is, if we are unclear on what to do with a passage, we must not move too quickly to what other ancient Near East sources have to say and assume that the biblical text must be understanding a concept in the same way. Talmon summarizes, "The elucidation of difficult terms and ideas must be achieved from the biblical books themselves, since they are the only reliable first-hand evidence which mirrors, albeit fragmentarily, the conceptual horizon of ancient Israel and the linguistic and literary modes in which it found its expression."[16] Talmon's concern echoes many of those who were responding in the second half of the twentieth century to the consequences of a diachronic (breaking the text into smaller units to study its development) rather than synchronic (reading the text as a unified whole) approach to reading Scripture. Talmon is pushing his audience to recognize the distinctive literary voice of the biblical witness.

Notably, in light of the growing momentum to identify the Hebrew epic with its ancient Near East counterparts (seen masterfully in Cross's *Canaanite Myth and Hebrew Epic*), Talmon insists that the distinctiveness of the Hebrew account is lost when scholars try too neatly to associate the Hebrew text with its temporal and geographic neighbors. He comments, "There can be no doubt that in the historiographies, the narratives, Psalms and even in the prophetic books we do encounter features which are characteristic of the epic genre. . . . However, these features are found also in literature to which the designation 'epic' cannot be applied."[17] Importantly for Talmon and for our own investigation, biblical Hebrew storytelling overlaps at times with other forms of ancient storytelling,

15. Cross, *Canaanite Myth and Hebrew Epic*; Talmon, "'Comparative Method,'" 320–56.
16. Talmon, "'Comparative Method,'" 350.
17. Talmon, "'Comparative Method,'" 354.

but that overlap should not be understood to mean that ancient Israelite authors lacked their own distinctive literary voice. "Of even greater import [than the shared epic features] is the following fact," Talmon stresses: "the outstanding predominance in the Bible of straightforward prose narration which fulfills the functions for which other literatures revert to the epic genre."[18] What is unique to ancient Israel's stories is the form they take.

Neither completely unlike nor simply adopting neighboring cultures' literary traditions, the storytelling we find in the Hebrew Bible is a new kind of storytelling—more like the modern novel than the ancient poetic epic.[19]

Recent scholarship continues to draw out the distinctiveness of ancient Israel's storytelling. While it's unsurprising that we find evidence of Mesopotamian and Ugaritic cultures,[20] among others, influencing the biblical Hebrew narrative, we also find in ancient Israel's literature "a highly creative matrix" between the older poetic literary representations and the influence of Mesopotamian culture found in the distinctive Hebraic prose tradition.[21] We find here a picture of an ingenious and creative artistry in biblical Hebrew narrative.

In my mind, one of the most evocative and profound elements of ancient Israel's storytelling has to do with its intended audience. Seth L. Sanders, in his 2009 work *The Invention of Hebrew*, makes the case for the development of the Hebrew language in biblical stories as carrying with it a sociopolitical force, in that "the Bible is the first text to address people as a public."[22] That is, in the neighboring ancient Near East cultures, stories of gods and humans are told to and in service of the political elite. Sanders argues that the distinctiveness of biblical Hebrew storytelling is a shift from stories of and for the elite class to the common people.[23] This distinctiveness gives Scripture much of its staying power in that it continues to speak to us, to *you*, generation after generation. I return to this unique second-person address to the whole people of God later in the

18. Talmon, "'Comparative Method,'" 354.

19. In *Biblical Narrative and the Death of the Rhapsode*, Robert S. Kawashima makes a case for the way that biblical narrative "anticipates formal features of the modern novel" by taking ancient Near East myth and epic forms and creating a new kind of storytelling (160).

20. Mesopotamia was home to the Babylonians and was located in what is now Iraq; Ugarit was home to the Amorites and was located in what is now Syria.

21. M. Smith, "Biblical Narrative between Ugaritic and Akkadian Literature—Part II," 202.

22. Sanders, *Invention of Hebrew*, 1.

23. Sanders, *Invention of Hebrew*, 3.

chapter on Deuteronomy, where we find the most evocative of addresses in the Shema: "Hear O Israel, the Lord our God, the Lord is one. *You* shall love the Lord *your* God with all *your* heart, and with all *your* soul, and with all *your* strength" (Deut. 6:4–5 NRSV).

For now, though, I want to reinforce the idea that the unique style of ancient Israel's storytelling has theological and, in turn, political motivation and impact. Sanders summarizes, "For over two thousand years, people have recognized the Bible as speaking directly to them, calling them to new forms of belonging that can threaten or transform the orders in which they find themselves. But no other Near Eastern texts talk like the Bible does; virtually all other literature was by and for scribes, courts, and kings. The Bible has meant far more than a court literature to many outside of courts."[24] The Bible's ability to speak in this new way has to do with the development of formalized alphabets that allowed scribes outside of the political elite to pass along stories of common people doing extraordinary things, like those accounts we find in the Pentateuch, in biblical histories, and in the prophets.[25]

Sanders, picking up on Auerbach's characterization of the Hebrew epic as "fraught with background," argues that through the stories of ancient Israel being told in the vernacular we find a new kind of storytelling for a different kind of audience. While history-writing existed in other ancient Near East cultures, particularly Mesopotamia, before and alongside biblical Hebrew narrative, the "persuasive style of biblical prose" introduces something new—especially in interweaving religious instruction (laws and rituals) into narrative form. This new form creates a dynamic reading experience for generations of readers to take up and read of the God who calls, covenants, liberates, and dwells among us. Each generation discerns how to keep the law, not through royal command, but through reflecting on a text in each new generation.[26] Ancient Israel's new kind of storytelling, available to layperson as well as priest and king, invites generations of readers into discerning how to respond anew to the God of Abraham, Isaac, and Jacob. Biblical Hebrew narrative is neither purely instructive

24. Sanders, *Invention of Hebrew*, xi.

25. Sanders, *Invention of Hebrew*, 7. Sanders argues that one of the major consequences of this shift from the elite to the everyday person means that the greatest of authorities, that from the realm of the divine, no longer requires mediation through the royal courts but can come through the common people and their language.

26. Sanders, *Invention of Hebrew*, 165.

nor purely entertainment, and its distinctiveness from other ancient texts rests in the invitation to all the people of God to wrestle with these stories to discern a proper response.[27] The stories are inseparable from the legislation—and the legislation cannot be understood without the stories.

Unlike a News Brief: Who? What? Why? Where? When? How?

In my early adulthood, I spent several years reading through as many nineteenth-century novels as I could get my hands on. The novel I returned to most frequently was Charlotte Brontë's *Jane Eyre*. Well known for the breaking of the fourth wall by directly addressing the reader, this novel invites readers into the inner thoughts, feelings, and turmoil of the story's heroine. I found the invitation into the most intimate and interior thoughts of Jane exhilarating. By the end of the novel, I felt both her despair and her delight pointedly.

What we find in biblical narrative is nothing like this experience. Earlier, I referred to biblical Hebrew narrative as possessing what's called a "paratactic" quality, where the story unfolds without much in the way of dependent clauses or details to fill in the scene. What we find in *Jane Eyre* is the opposite: a hypotactic style where one big idea may find an abundance of subordinate clauses describing the view, the emotion, the inner thoughts. Sometimes we know more about what Jane thinks and feels than we know about what actually happens!

On the other side, biblical Hebrew narrative may carry with it the matter-of-fact tone that we find when we look at our news feed or listen to a news brief on our favorite podcast. The tone feels similar: *this* happened, and then *this*, and finally ***this***. But the content is different. The general news arc is to tell us what happened, where it happened, how it happened, and who it happened to before exploring the intentions behind the action—that is, why it happened (or why it *might* have).

In biblical narrative, we are not frequently given the *why* aside from the narrative summaries that often begin with an editorial insertion explaining the etiology (origin) of a name or practice. Narrative summaries are not

27. Sternberg notes of the distinction between ancient Israel's literature and the literature of its neighbors: "If anything can account for such a radical break in aesthetics, this is I believe the coincident break with pagan metaphysics" (Sternberg, *Poetics of Biblical Narrative*, 232). In other words, the distinctive style is linked to a distinctive view of divine workings in the world.

quite like the breaking of the fourth wall that we find in *Jane Eyre*. Instead of speaking directly to the reader, the biblical narrator offers a wrap-up of what has just been narrated, often linking a single story to the broader story of a key figure or offering an explanation for how a tradition or place name arose from a narrated event. Many biblical scholars identify narrative summaries as later additions that weave together older stories into a cohesive narrative fabric. We find a characteristic editorial comment in Genesis 32:32: "Therefore to this day the Israelites do not eat the thigh muscle that is on the hip socket, because he struck Jacob on the hip socket at the thigh muscle" (NRSV). Yet these kinds of comments do not exactly offer us help as we try to answer the "why" of this pericope (a small, self-contained set of verses). Why did Jacob wrestle with this mysterious angel-man? Surely it wasn't simply to help us with a dietary practice. The comments offer us a kind of resolution to the story but not an explanation.

The brevity we find in the Pentateuch's narratives directly impacts our task as readers in making sense of the text. Sternberg helpfully draws out this responsibility when he asks what the goal of biblical narration might be.

> [This is] a fundamental question that students of the Bible would do well to pose loudly and sharply: The question of the narrative as a functional structure, a means to a communicative end, a transaction between the narrator and the audience on whom he wishes to produce a certain effect by way of certain strategies. Like all social discourse, biblical narrative is oriented to an addressee and regulated by a purpose or a set of purposes involving the addressee. Hence our primary business as readers is to make purposive sense of it, so as to explain the *what*'s and the *how*'s in terms of the *why*'s of communication.[28]

In other words, stories are written in a particular way as an act of communication. Brontë's choice to share Jane Eyre's interior world was an intentional one, an invitation for a certain kind of engagement. This form of narration does not mean that readers will, in fact, engage that structure as intended or even do it well, but it is a good reminder that what we find in a story's shape is an invitation to engage in a certain way. In biblical narrative, we are not given many interior motives or exterior details to draw out the

28. Sternberg, *Poetics of Biblical Narrative*, 1.

scene (e.g., What did the Jabbok River's banks look like as Jacob wrestled with the angel? Was it sandy? Muddy? Were there flies? Did Jacob grunt? Did the angel break a sweat? Was the angel annoyed that Jacob wouldn't release him until he got his blessing?).

Consider the story of the blasphemer in Leviticus 24:10–23, which disrupts a description of maintenance of the tabernacle:

> A man whose mother was an Israelite and whose father was an Egyptian came out among the people of Israel; and the Israelite woman's son and a certain Israelite began fighting in the camp. The Israelite woman's son blasphemed the Name in a curse. And they brought him to Moses—now his mother's name was Shelomith, daughter of Dibri, of the tribe of Dan—and they put him in custody, until the decision of the Lord should be made clear to them.
>
> The Lord said to Moses, saying: Take the blasphemer outside the camp; and let all who were within hearing lay their hands on his head, and let the whole congregation stone him. (24:10–14 NRSV)

Following this brief narrative action, Moses addresses the people as God commands him, explaining that a person who curses God will die and that a punishment should fit the crime (i.e., an eye for an eye, a tooth for a tooth). After Moses's address, the story concludes: "Moses spoke thus to the people of Israel; and they took the blasphemer outside the camp, and stoned him to death. The people of Israel did as the Lord had commanded Moses" (24:23 NRSV).

Take a moment and read back through the story. What is the basic narrative arc? What information is missing? Is there a reason, do you think, that we are not told the blasphemer's name? Or why this is one of only two narrative sections in the whole book of Leviticus (the first being Lev. 8–10)? For both Jacob's wrestling and Leviticus's blasphemer, we are left to respond to these stories imaginatively—taking up the narrative's bare bones and giving them flesh.

Somewhere between the Truth and the Whole Truth

One of the most readily evident elements of slowly reading through a biblical story is not what is present but what is absent. Frequently, the stories seem to be missing pertinent details that would help make sense of the narrative. Danish theologian Søren Kierkegaard's *Fear and Trembling* begins with four vignettes based on the Genesis 22:1–19 account of Abraham's binding of Isaac. These imaginative renderings of the story fill in the unnarrated interior emotions and exterior elements that are lacking in the text. What follows is a portion of the first vignette, which demonstrates the ways that Kierkegaard responds to the brief pericope:

> Abraham arose betimes, he had the asses saddled, left his tent, and Isaac with him, but Sarah looked out of the window after them until they had passed down the valley and she could see them no more. They rode in silence for three days. . . . He left the young men behind and went on alone with Isaac beside him up to the mountain. But Abraham said to himself, "I will not conceal from Isaac whither this course leads him." He stood still, he laid his hand upon the head of Isaac in benediction, and Isaac bowed to receive the blessing. And Abraham's face was fatherliness, his look was mild, his speech encouraging. But Isaac was unable to understand him, his soul could not be exalted; he embraced Abraham's knees, he fell at his feet imploringly, he begged for his young life, for the fair hope of his future, he called to mind the joy in Abraham's house, he called to mind the sorrow and loneliness. Then Abraham lifted up the boy, he walked with him by his side, and his talk was full of comfort and exhortation. But Isaac could not understand him. He climbed Mount Moriah, but Isaac understood him not. Then for an instant he turned away from him, and when Isaac again saw Abraham's face it was changed, his glance was wild, his form was horror. He seized Isaac by the throat, threw him to the ground, and said, "Stupid boy, dost thou then suppose that I am thy father? I am an idolater. Dost thou suppose that this is God's bidding? No, it is my desire." Then Isaac trembled and cried out in his terror, "O God in heaven, have compassion upon me. God of Abraham, have compassion upon me. If I have no father upon earth, be Thou my father!" But Abraham in a low voice said to himself, "O Lord in heaven, I thank Thee. After all it is better for him to believe that I am a monster, rather than that he should lose faith in Thee."[29]

Notice how Kierkegaard is faithful to the biblical account while boldly imagining the interior life of the characters, as well as how the event might have played out. Most notably, Kierkegaard gives Isaac speech when the

29. Kierkegaard, *Fear and Trembling*, 38–40.

biblical story leaves him mute throughout the whole proceedings. Maybe we are tempted to believe that if the biblical account does not give Isaac speech, then we should not allow for it, but this temptation undercuts the idea that the text is a form a communication, a reading event, that finds meaning only through participation with a reader. The brevity of the story does not cut off meaning but instead leaves us as readers to discern what portions of the unsaid might enrich our understanding of the story.

The idea of exploring the unsaid portions of a biblical story can be seen in the Black preaching tradition of the sanctified imagination. Wil Gafney defines "the sanctified imagination" as "the fertile creative space where preacher-interpreter enters the text, particularly the spaces in the text, and fills them out with missing details: names, back stories, detailed descriptions of the scene and characters, and so on."[30] Here we see this same impulse of invitation through preaching and inviting hearers to enter more deeply into the text.

Within biblical scholarship, there are temptations to explain away the brief nature of biblical Hebrew narrative with its stops and starts, omissions, and repetitions as a result of a historically developed and fragmented text. Arguably, no portion of the Bible has experienced this kind of treatment more thoroughly or famously than the Pentateuch has with the documentary hypothesis, which divides (and then frequently subdivides) the five books into four primary sources, which are stitched together sometimes crudely to result in the form we now have.[31] And, while the Pentateuch's formation very likely *was* a compilation of stories, songs, and religious instructions stitched together over time, we should be wary of identifying the historical development of texts like the Pentateuch as being without artistry simply because it was not written in the same manner as we are accustomed. As Adele Berlin, Hebrew scholar and one of the foremost advocates for literary interpretation, insists, the "fragmenting of the narrative into sources . . . ignores the rhetorical and poetic features which bind the narrative together."[32]

When reading Kierkegaard's imagined retelling of Genesis 22, we may wonder if he took a few too many liberties—maybe reading content into

30. Gafney, *Womanist Midrash*, 3.

31. As an approachable example of how these sources are divided up, see Friedman, *Bible with Sources Revealed*.

32. Berlin, *Poetics and Interpretation*, 121.

places where the narrative was simply silent because there was nothing to be told. Are there times when a lack of information is not an invitation but merely not important to note? How do we know which it is? In an attempt to delineate meaningful narrative blanks from unimportant ones, some scholars distinguish between silences and gaps to differentiate places where information is not provided because it is unimportant (silences) and where absent information importantly invites readers to fill it in (gaps).[33] I find this distinction less than helpful for a number of reasons. The first reason is simply a matter of semantics, since some use the language of "gaps" for any portion of a narrative where information is not present, whereas others distinguish between the two. The second and more central criticism here is that readers often are not immediately in a position to determine what constitutes a productive narrative "gap" versus a fruitless narrative "silence." When information is not given to readers, the reader must *discern* the opportunities for wonder and imagine what might fill the vacancy. Finally, what constitutes a beneficial opportunity for information-filling depends on the reader. It might be unimportant for one reader to imagine the terrain of Abraham and Isaac's journey, whereas an avid hiker's imagination may be enlivened by envisioning the narrative scene.

In my mind, the most helpful delineation for navigating the Pentateuch's brevity, and the brevity in the broader biblical narrative as well, is the distinction Sternberg makes between the truth and the whole truth of a narrative.[34] This interpretive space between truth in part and in whole rests on the ambiguity of the text wherein "the Bible allows itself considerable room between elucidation and implication."[35] As readers of biblical narrative, we elucidate meaning from the text. For example, Abraham brought Isaac to Mount Moriah in obedience, but God supplied an alternate sacrifice. Jacob wrestled all night with a strange figure on his way to meet with his aggrieved brother Esau and received a wounding blow to his hip. The Israelites have a serious grumbling and doubting problem as they wander

33. In Sternberg, a "gap" is defined as "a lack of information about the world . . . contrived by temporal displacement." The gap is filled when temporal continuity is restored to the narrative. Gaps are understood as offering relevancy to the narrative when filled. A "blank," in distinction, is omitted information that does not prove relevant to the text (Sternberg, *Poetics of Biblical Narrative*, 235–36). Here is a silly but helpful example of a blank: it makes no difference to our task as readers whether Moses had a sweet tooth.

34. Sternberg, *Poetics of Biblical Narrative*, 230–63.

35. Sternberg, *Poetics of Biblical Narrative*, 233.

the wilderness after God liberates them from enslavement in Egypt. The biblical narrator proves reliable in the contours of these stories, allowing readers to access the truth of the story.

But elucidation is not where the readers' work necessarily ends in reading a brief and ambiguous story. Implication, what Sternberg terms "the whole truth," requires inference and gap-filling. This whole truth is the realm of plurality and instability, unlike the work of elucidation. Sternberg comments, "The narrator may play games with the whole truth for the pleasure and benefit of the cunning few, but he must communicate the truth in a fashion accessible to all."[36] To return to the earlier examples, we do not know how Abraham *felt* about God's directive to sacrifice his only son or *how* Jacob wrestled with the angel (say, with strength and athleticism or speed and technique), and we don't have a *full description* of the conditions of living a nomadic life in the wilderness.

Sternberg describes this movement from the truth to a (more) whole truth as closing a gap in the narrative, wherein the gap's ambiguity is replaced by an inferred significance. In resolving the ambiguity, one does not smooth over and forget the cause for the gap so much as elevate it as an important piece of information that gives us a more robust narrative. In the abstract, this idea can seem cryptic, but we will see in our ensuing reading of Nadab and Abihu's demise in Leviticus 10 just how this play of gap-filling enriches our reading of a brief story.

Case Study: Leviticus 10:1–7

In the book of Leviticus, two narrative sections stand in contrast to the instructions on worship that define the book. The first narrative portion is found in Leviticus 8–10, where the Aaronide priesthood is established. The second, as we have seen, is found in Leviticus 24, where amid the Holiness Code is a story about the judgment of a man who blasphemes against the Lord. While both of these portions offer us opportunities to see brevity at work in biblical narrative, particularly in each story's action, I will focus here on the earlier narrative portion.

In Leviticus 8–9, all seems to be going well. In Leviticus 8, Aaron and his sons are ceremonially washed and are dressed in ornate vestments,

36. Sternberg, *Poetics of Biblical Narrative*, 235.

and then they offer a sin offering and burnt offerings. Following the sacrifices, Aaron and his sons are anointed with the same oil that consecrated the tabernacle, holy vessels, and altar. Moses then commands the men to wait for seven days and nights and not leave the tabernacle in order for their consecration as priests to be complete. In Leviticus 9, with the consecration complete on the eighth day, Aaron adopts the role of high priest (replacing the interim priestly role Moses had taken) and with his sons offers sin and burnt offerings. He then makes collective sacrifice for all the people, fulfilling the role of priesthood for all the people of God. The scene culminates when Moses and Aaron exit the tabernacle. As they offer blessings to the people, the glory of the Lord appears, and from this presence a mysterious fire consumes all the elements on the altar, signifying God's satisfaction with the offerings Aaron and his sons have prepared. In response to this spectacular scene, all those who witnessed it call out in praise and fall to the ground in awe.

As we enter the next pericope, we find a very different kind of narrative:

> And the sons of Aaron—Nadab and Abihu—each took his censer and they set fire in them and they set incense upon the fire and they offered a strange[37] fire before the LORD which was not commanded to them. And fire went out from before the LORD and it consumed them and they died before the LORD. And Moses said to Aaron that which the LORD spoke, saying: Among those close to me, I will be shown as holy and before the presence of all the people I will be honored. And Aaron was silent. And Moses called for Mishael and Elzaphan, sons of Uzziel, uncle of Aaron, and he said to them: Come near and take your brothers away from the holy place to the outside of the camp. And they drew near and took them with their tunics to outside the camp, just as Moses directed. And Moses said to Aaron and to Eleazar and to Ithamar, his sons: The hair on your head is not to hang loose and your garments are not to be torn and you will not die and before all the congregation he will not be angry. And all your brothers, all the houses of

37. Some translators choose more specific translations for the word *zar*, making a more value-laden judgment of inappropriate ritual action, but I am translating *zar* simply as "strange." These other translations include the following: "impermissible" (Gerstenberger, *Leviticus*), "unauthorized" (ESV; NIV; Milgrom, *Leviticus*), "unholy" (NRSV), "wrong kind" (NLT). The Hebrew word itself is used both to modify an object and to signify a person who is outside the community (non-Israelite) or a person who is not in a proper role (a layperson performing priestly duties). When this event is recalled in Num. 3:5–10, it is used to justify why the Aaronide priests (and not strangers/outsiders) may come near holy things. I am retaining the more open-ended connotations of "stranger" in my choice of translation.

> Israel, will weep regarding the burning which the Lord burned. And from the entrance of the tent of meeting they will not go out lest they die, for the anointing oil of the Lord is upon you and they acted according to the word of Moses. (Lev. 10:1–7)

The translation I offer here is not beautiful. It does not render the artistry we find in the Hebrew narrative into a similarly artistic English translation. In my mind, the King James Version (KJV) also renders this pericope exceptionally well. As I do at times throughout this book, in lieu of the most beautiful or even literal rendering, I offer a translation that reveals some of the wordplay, ambiguity, and gaps that are often removed, clarified, or filled in by many translations. And, of course, what I offer remains *a translation*, with interpretive choices of my own at play. The choices here are guided by an interest in helping non-Hebrew readers to see "under the hood," as it were, in ways that might not always be readily available. One way to do this same kind of work without access to the Hebrew is to compare various translations of one biblical story, taking note of where the translations diverge.[38]

Returning to the story of Nadab and Abihu, notice that we find a very different kind of story than we expected. After the miraculous appearing of the glory of God with the consecration of Aaron and his sons to serve in the role of priests, Leviticus 10:1–2 startles readers out of a posture of reverence and into one of fear, very likely mirroring the mood of those within the story. This is hinted at beginning in verse 3, with Aaron's noted silence. Consider the flow of the first three verses, where the majority of the narrative action takes place (indicated in italics):

> *And the sons of Aaron*—Nadab and Abihu—*each took his censer*
> *and they set fire in them*
> *and they set incense upon it*
> *and they offered a strange fire* before the Lord which was not commanded to them.

38. There are many ways to compare translations. With free online sources, you can compare a number of translations of the same passage. Or you could purchase a few different translations of the Bible and then read them side by side. I would recommend comparing the KJV, NRSV (or NRSVue), NIV (or TNIV), CSB, and The Message, but there is no limit to the number or type of translations you could compare with this kind of exercise.

And fire went out from before the LORD
and it consumed them
and they died before the LORD.
And Moses said to Aaron that which the LORD spoke, saying: Among those close to me, I will be shown as holy and before the presence of all the people I will be honored.
And Aaron was silent.

The story begins with Aaron's sons each taking their censers and ends with them burned alive and Aaron silent, all within a handful of lines. What do we make of such a startling reversal—from God's blessing to God's wrath—in such quick succession? Why are we given two chapters of rather uneventful narrative as Aaron and his sons properly adopt the priestly roles and only two verses in which a cryptic transgression leads to a literal consuming fire?

The task of attending to the gaps of a spare story like this can be frustrating. The movement toward a more "whole truth" picture of this story feels risky, and the work of inference feels subjective. At the heart of my argument in this chapter we find the heart, I think, of such a sparely wrought story as this one. The ambiguity of the *why* questions serves not as an impediment but as an invitation to enter the imaginative space of these brief stories. A story like this one leaves room for readers to wonder and wander through the narrative world.

Here is what we can elucidate easily from the text. The two sons of Aaron, Nadab and Abihu, undertake an offering in their new vocation as priests on the same day that their father, now high priest, made offerings pleasing to the Lord. All the camp was in awe of God's glory and humbled by the majesty of it. The two sons each take their own censer, place fire (think, a coal) in it, and then place incense atop it. Some of you may be familiar with this practice if you attend a church that regularly or on special liturgical days of the year places incense in a censer or thurible that a priest or deacon uses to bless instruments and parishioners during a church service. We are told, however, that what Nadab and Abihu offer to the Lord is not right; it is "strange," which is sometimes translated as "unholy," "unauthorized," or simply "wrong" in Leviticus 10:1:

> And [they] offered *strange fire* before the Lord, which he commanded them not. (KJV)
>
> And they offered *unauthorized fire* before the Lord, contrary to his command. (NIV)
>
> In this way, they disobeyed the Lord by burning before him *the wrong kind of fire*, different than he had commanded. (NLT)
>
> And they offered *unholy fire* before the Lord, such as he had not commanded them. (NRSV)

The action of offering the strange fire was an act of disobedience. Immediately thereafter the fire of the Lord, the same one that consumed the offering made at the end of Leviticus 9, now consumes not a pleasing offering but disobedient priests. The fire blazed forward, surrounded them, and killed them. All of these events occur in two verses. The remaining five verses that follow, and the extended dialogue that takes up the rest of the chapter, speak to the aftermath of this action. Moses speaks; Aaron is silent. Moses directs; Aaron's sons' corpses are carried outside the camp. Moses tells Aaron and his family they are not to mourn; they do as Moses commands.

I imagine, though, that this elucidation of "what happened" does not offer us a satisfactory answer to why such a terrifying story appears in such short form, after a magnificent scene of God's glory on the same day, in one of the few narrative portions of a book dominated by religious instruction. We are not told why this happened. We're left with many *why* questions: Why these two sons? Why the use of the cryptic word "strange" instead of a more specific adjective as the clue for the disobedience? Why such a brutal response, and why did the response come so quickly? Why is Moses not troubled? Why is Aaron silent? And on it goes.

We have a number of hints to help us interrogate the gaps from this story. I want to point to a couple of them to show how we are invited into the interpretive work of inference and how it will move us toward a more whole truth. First, notice that the text tells us that "each took his censer" at the start of the scene. When we are given so little to go on, the fact that we are not told that they took censers more generally or that these censers are specifically for use with offerings gives us pause. (Exod. 38:3 tells us about bronze censers made specifically for the altar.) That these censers are Nadab's and Abihu's respectively invites us to wonder about this choice. Did the men realize they were using the wrong censers? Were their personal censers also bronze? In such a spare story, we are told not only that Nadab and Abihu each used "a censor" (which would be one word in Hebrew) but even that "each took his censer," signaled with the additional word *ish*, which here functions to emphasize the distinction between the two censer's possessors.[39] That is, we are invited here to ask what is going on: Why would each take up his own censer? Why does the narrator find it important to include this detail? In a story with so few details, the addition of seemingly unnecessary words intimates that the storyteller is leaving hints for readers to take up.

The translation "each took his own" also offers us an opportunity to see the value in reading multiple translations of a single text in order to spot literary artistry even without training in biblical Hebrew. The following are translations of the first part of Leviticus 10:1 from a number of well-known Bible translations:

> Aaron's sons Nadab and Abihu *each took his own firepan* . . . (CSB)
>
> Now Nadab and Abihu, the sons of Aaron, *each took his censer* . . . (ESV)
>
> And Nadab and Abihu, the sons of Aaron, *took each of them his censer* (JPS)
>
> And Nadab and Abihu, the sons of Aaron, *took either of them his censer* . . . (KVJ)
>
> Aaron's sons Nadab and Abihu *took their censers* . . . (NIV)
>
> Aaron's sons Nadab and Abihu *put coals of fire in their incense burners* . . . (NLT)
>
> Now Aaron's sons, Nadab and Abihu, *each took his censer* . . . (NRSV)

39. The form of "censer" used here is singular ("his censer"), meaning that each one took his censer. Use of the plural would suggest that the censers are to be understood collectively. It seems important to understand each censer as being associated distinctively with Nadab or Abihu.

Notice the shift halfway through these examples from the singular "censer" to plural "censers." Readers don't need to perform an online search to find a word-for-word Hebrew-to-English translation to see the differences between English translations here. These differences alert us to a place of ambiguity, where some translators chose to use a singular term, even if it creates a less smooth translation, and other translators simply used the plural "their censers." We find an opportunity here to ask, Does it make a difference if each took his own censer?

Nadab and Abihu just spent an intense week with the rest of their family within the confines of the tent of meeting. Now, eight days after they first entered, they watch as their dad takes on the formal role of high priest. Nadab and Abihu help to bleed out and dismember the young lamb and calf. They bring the blood offering to their father as many look on. Aaron marks all sides of the altar with blood. Then, as the sons bring the offerings piece by piece to the altar, their dad burns the pieces on the altar. The smell is mouthwatering, then pungent. Smoke rises up from the altar into the realms of the heavens. They and their dad continue this dance of sacrifice on behalf of the entire camp; people look on with expectation and gratitude. After those first days of doubt and grumbling in the wilderness, Nadab and Abihu finally feel a sense of purpose as they have an important role to play. Their dad and uncle return from within the tent of meeting, and their dad blesses the people. Suddenly the most awesome and terrifying scene unfolds as the glory of God appears and consumes all that remains of the altar. As the people begin to pick themselves up from where they fell in worship and wipe off the dust, Nadab catches the eye of one onlooker and sees the hopeful look in return. Abihu catches the look of adoration and respect from one of the well-known elders who carefully brings himself to his feet. Now it is Nadab and Abihu's turn to show their value, as their father has just done. Maybe their hearts swelled with pride, ready to prove themselves worthy of their birthright. Maybe they are impatient with the older generation, ready to steal the spotlight. Or, maybe they are simply distracted with mixed feelings of exhaustion and glee, so they hastily look to themselves for what to do next. What is clear is that something goes wrong in this moment; our first hint of it is not the "strange" fire they offer or the note that they did what was not commanded. Instead, it comes by way of the small additional note that *each* man took his own censer and went through the standard procedure of preparing incense for the offering. This additional word is the minor chord that hints at what is to come. The individuation in choice of instrument alerts us to a much greater breach.

One interesting reading of this story is found in *Ritual Words and Narrative Worlds in the Book of Leviticus*, wherein Bryan D. Bibb identifies the narrated demise of Nadab and Abihu as exemplifying ritual failure in Leviticus. As Bibb begins to analyze what exactly went wrong in Nadab and Abihu's offering, he first asks whether their actions can be deemed a willful breach or should instead be understood as an accidental "misfire."[40] Bibb deduces from the previous positive narration of the establishment of the Aaronide priesthood that a willful rebellion appears less than likely, and equally unlikely is an obvious ineptitude on the part of the priests. Instead, the most likely explanation for ritual failure is the ambiguous nature of the ritual system itself.[41]

Through a close literary reading of Leviticus 10:1–7 within its broader context, Bibb recognizes the radical shift in tone between this pericope and its surrounding narration and legal legislation. In fact, the preceding narrative sets up the reader for "the best chance they will ever have of getting it right," having just been given proper instruction for the priestly rituals.[42] This narrative subverts a reader's expectations that priests will properly execute the ritual when it depicts the priests getting it entirely wrong. The meaning of Leviticus 10 resides within the ambiguity of their failure and the gaps in explanation. "This story is itself *about* gap-filling and its attendant danger and frustration."[43] Meaning is not found in the filling of gaps; the meaning *is* the gaps.

The narrative functions within the legal text both to demonstrate the function of the law in protecting others from an outcome like Nadab and Abihu's—a function Bibb identifies in Moses's "flurry of activity" in the second half of Leviticus 10, as God works to protect against this occurring again—and to demonstrate the provisional character of the priestly legislation because situations will always arise in the gaps of legislation.[44] The one assurance the reader is offered in Leviticus 10 is that God's actions

40. Bibb, *Ritual Words*, 116.
41. Bibb, *Ritual Words*, 116.
42. Bibb, *Ritual Words*, 117.
43. Bibb, *Ritual Words*, 117.
44. Bibb, *Ritual Words*, 129.

are just, even as they are also elusive. That is, the gaps are a human-error issue and not a question of God's own character.

In this spare story, each word carries with it a force not found in more robust storytelling. Bibb may well be right that the ambiguity of the story signals the ambiguity of the sacrificial act for Nadab and Abihu. But I don't think the purpose for the ambiguity ends. We are invited to wonder at this strange fire that each man gives in his own censer and the swift judgment of this action by God, who earlier that day seemed so pleased. This kind of story invites us into the narrative world, bringing it to life through our own wandering in it. We help make a story like this one a place to occupy creatively, contemplatively, and prayerfully because it leaves us so much room to bring ourselves into it. We are offered a story to contemplate and to wonder at the actions unsaid and the interior thoughts and emotions unspoken. This is the invitation of spare stories.

Conclusion

I realize there may be some anxiety in this approach related to how we place guardrails on our reading so that we don't veer off the path into unhelpful or even inappropriate interpretations. This anxiety is legitimate, especially because we have seen how the Bible has been weaponized in ways contrary to the good news of the gospel and, on the other side, how the Bible can be made to say all kinds of things that feel disconnected from its central message. And while there is no interpretive key to assure we get the story "right," we can keep in mind a few principles. First, one Jewish scholar helpfully speaks about the "givenness" of the biblical text through things like recurring words, stylistic choices, and editorial arrangement.[45] This means that the text is not a blank slate but gives us material to engage with, material that speaks to how this text should be read. Readers who are attentive to things like what we talk about in this book—pacing, characterization, complexity, and so on—will have a kind of interpretive path to walk down. These features do not function quite like guardrails, but they can still give us an indication of when a reading goes astray.

Second, I had a professor once speak about the ability of the text to "bite back."[46] An attentive reader, like a good conversation partner, will

45. Fishbane, *Biblical Text and Texture*, xii.
46. Credit to Iain Provan.

be aware of when they aren't listening well to what the text brings to the interpretive table. Have you ever been in a Bible study where someone proposes a reading of a passage and then another astute participant notes that the proposed reading doesn't engage with the idea in the next line? I have had that experience even in preparing this book, when I go to a story sure I know what I am going to get out of it, only to realize that a certain phrase or action pushes back on my interpretation.

This picture of the Bible study brings me to a final consideration regarding correct interpretation. Reading Scripture has never been intended to be done in isolation. The Bible is a communal text; it was compiled by a community, it is about a communal life around a communal God, and it has been passed down generation to generation by communities of people. We can best know if we have completely gone off the rails if our interpretation goes against how Scripture reads itself intertextually and how communities of faith have received these texts. Here I offer my boldest take, which is that we cannot be good readers of Scripture if we are not in conversation with other readers—in our present faith communities or in those generations of faithful people who passed down these stories to us. Things like the Apostles' Creed and the Nicene Creed also help us stay on track, keeping us from straying too far away from the communal witness about the God who has been spoken about in the life of Israel and revealed most fully in Jesus. It is in a community of readers that the invitation to read offers us both the richest experience and the best protection against getting too far offtrack.

CHAPTER 3

Pacing

Introduction

Pacing serves as one of the key tools for a storyteller. Across genres, the artistic choice to speed up or slow down at central moments of a story can draw attention toward a particular emotion, action, or motive. It can also draw attention away from the central action to allow for inference, suspense, or wonder. We see pacing at work in all sorts of ways. Often in novels we find that pacing plays a pivotal role as one chapter ends and the next begins, skipping over days, years, and sometimes even generations. In movies and television, linear jumps are frequently made from one scene or season to the next, where the show might jump ahead in time and then use flashbacks to fill the audience in on the proper sequence of events. Similarly, we have all likely experienced time slowing down in a story, maybe through the inner monologue of a character, extended reflections by a narrator, or a scene where a character's life flashes before their eyes, triggered by a gunshot, glaring headlights, or some other sign of an upcoming, devastating event. While pacing serves as a crucial part of storytelling, one with which we are well familiar, its role in helping to focus our attention or leave certain particulars shrouded in mystery is a form of artistry to which we aren't always attentive, particularly in the ancient stories of the Bible, where we may not expect to find the same type of artistry at work as is evident in many of our more contemporary examples.

In this chapter, I show how the pacing of biblical Hebrew narrative invites readers into a particular, and particularly evocative, reading event. The protracted genealogies and exacting descriptions of worship spaces and practices are well-known features of the first five books, most notoriously in the less-often-read books of Leviticus and Numbers. Notably, the more well-known scenes of narrative action—like Cain murdering his brother, the tower of Babel, and Jacob's wrestling on the banks of the Jabbok—occupy much less space and have fewer narrative details than the passages surrounding them. Why is it that the most climactic and central moments of ancient Israel's identity frequently take up significantly less space than more mundane events, descriptions, and instructions?

Pacing in Storytelling

In literature, we speak about the pace of any given story most easily by contrasting "clock" or "actual" time with "narrated" time.[1] Understanding clock time is rather straightforward. It takes me seven minutes on a given morning to drive from my house to the nearest coffee shop. Clock time is fixed. The clock tracks at regular intervals the linear movement of time as I put my car in gear and make my way to my destination. Narrated time, on the other hand, is much more variable. I could account for my drive to the coffee shop in an elaborate short story about my journey across town where I hit every possible red light, take note of the weather, describe the faces of other drivers, detail my inner thoughts, share the state of my fuel gauge, and offer an extended reflection on how I would save money if I brewed coffee at home—and on it might go. I could also simply narrate: "I drove to the coffee shop today." Narrated time can expand into an elaborate and lengthy treatise or speak of a seven-minute event in seven words.

1. "Narrated time" is just one of many ways to speak of this phenomenon. Shlomith Rimmon-Kenan speaks of what I am calling narrated time as "text-time" (Rimmon-Kenan, *Narrative Fiction*, 44). Shimon Bar-Efrat, writing specifically on biblical Hebrew narrative, uses the terms "narrated time" and "narrative time" in the way I employ "clock time" (Bar-Efrat, *Narrative Art*, 141). As an example from the broader field of literary studies, H. Porter Abbott, in the *Cambridge Introduction to Narrative*, refers to clock time in the same way as I do, while referring to narrated time as "narrative time," noting that "both of these kinds of time have been with us as far back as history can trace. We have always been aware of the recurring cycles of the sun, moon, and seasons, and at the same time we have always been shaping and reshaping time as a succession of events, that is, as narrative." Abbott, *Cambridge Introduction to Narrative*, 5.

There are many ways to think about how time works in narrative. When we're discussing pacing, maybe the best way to think of its function is in terms of a spectrum with the standard narrated time in a work serving as a baseline with the possibility of a story speeding up or slowing down, both of which disrupt the narrative flow.[2] The narrative becomes more truncated as pacing accelerates, reaching its height when a portion of time is entirely omitted; the narrative can also go the other direction, expanding to the point of pausing time all together.[3] We can think of the relationship of a story's standard narrated time to the speeding up or slowing down of pacing in this way:

pause ← *slow down* ← **standard narrated time** → *speed up* → omission

In biblical narrative, the most quintessential example of narrative deceleration can be found in narrative comments that summarize or reflect on a narrative scene. A simple example can be found in Genesis 12's calling of Abram, where we read:

> Now the Lord said to Abram, "Go from your country and your kindred and your father's house to the land that I will show you. I will make of you a great nation, and I will bless you, and make your name great, so that you will be a blessing. I will bless those who bless you, and the one who curses you I will curse; and in you all the families of the earth shall be blessed." So Abram went, as the Lord had told him; and Lot went with him. *Abram was seventy-five years old when he departed from Haran.* (Gen. 12:1–4 NRSV)

See how the narrative possesses a temporal pacing from one action to another until disrupted in the second half of verse 4? The comment about Abram's age disrupts the pacing of the narrative to insert a comment that fills in details of the story, but it also takes us out of the story. Why might it be valuable for the narrator to pause here and take note of Abram's age?

2. One literary theorist speaks of this standard narrated time as a kind of "overall rhythm" or "norm tempo" that serves as the baseline for any change in pacing within a scene. Bal, *Narratology*, 99–100.

3. I am making use of Rimmon-Kenan's discussion of duration with the regular pace of story as a "norm" with the possibility of "acceleration and deceleration." Rimmon-Kenan, *Narrative Fiction*, 53–54.

In the same chapter, the pacing moves in the other direction. A rather glaring (and troubling) narrative omission occurs as the story speeds up and glosses over seemingly key events as Abram and Sarai travel south from Haran toward Egypt:

> Now there was a famine in the land. So Abram went down to Egypt to reside there as an alien, for the famine was severe in the land. When he was about to enter Egypt, he said to his wife Sarai, "I know well that you are a woman beautiful in appearance; and when the Egyptians see you, they will say, 'This is his wife'; then they will kill me, but they will let you live. Say you are my sister, so that it may go well with me because of you, and that my life may be spared on your account." [___] When Abram entered Egypt the Egyptians saw that the woman was very beautiful. When the officials of Pharaoh saw her, they praised her to Pharaoh. And the woman was taken into Pharaoh's house. And for her sake he dealt well with Abram; and he had sheep, oxen, male donkeys, male and female slaves, female donkeys, and camels. (Gen. 12:10–16 NRSV)

Key information is omitted between the end of verse 13 and start of verse 14, marked by my inclusion of the brackets. Easily overlooked, the gap between Abraham's instructions and the entrance into Egypt leaves readers to infer Sarai's subservient acceptance of Abram's suggestion—or possibly a lovers' quarrel. The narrative itself skips ahead without a hint of what occurred in this unnarrated time.

Another example of the impact of pacing, this time with a journey toward rather than away from Haran, can be seen in Genesis 28–29, as Jacob journeys north away from his home after receiving through deception the blessing that belonged to his brother. First, we are told in verse 10 that "Jacob left Beer-sheba and went toward Haran" and then in the next verse that "he came to a certain place and stayed there for the night, because the sun had set" (28:10–11 NRSV). The distance covered between these two verses is approximately fifty miles. Already, we have a scene jump between the start of this story and the arrival at "a certain place," a place that would come to be known as Bethel. This travel north races along even more rapidly when, after Jacob dreams of a ladder with heavenly beings ascending and descending, he sets out the next morning: "Then Jacob went on his journey, and came to the land of the people of the east" (29:1 NRSV). In this verse, Jacob travels another 450 miles or so north into the region of Paddan-Aram.

Though a contemporary movie scene may suggest a long distance traveled with a screen fading to black or plane wheels screeching on a tarmac, in the biblical text we are not given any indicator of the distance traveled before Jacob arrived in "the land of the people in the east." And, unlike in modern stories, where we can pick up on these gapped travel days because we are familiar with the distances—say, by ship from London to New York, by plane from Los Angeles to Seoul, or by foot from Istanbul to Athens—in the biblical text we can miss the magnitude of the distance traveled if we are unfamiliar with ancient Near Eastern geography.[4] The vast journey can all the more be easily missed because of the stark contrast between standard narrated time and narrated space and the contrast between narrated time and the actual time it would take for such a journey. That is, we cover a lot of literal ground and many months of travel without so much as a nod to the extent of the journey, and we'll miss these details unless we're familiar with the geography.

It might be easy to dismiss this change in pacing as a simple by-product of any narration, where irrelevant or unimportant details are necessarily omitted sometimes, but I think the biblical narratives invite us to give the authors' narrative choices greater attention. Why do the biblical narrators, who generally write so sparely, include the details they do when they slow down the standard pace of narration? And why do they skip over seemingly important details at other points in the narrative? While not all changes in pacing will yield the same bounty of interpretive riches, we may find ourselves surprised at how often these changes do, in fact, enrich our reading and readerly imaginations.

Imagine Jacob for a moment. An unmediated divine vision has just been given to him, the newly minted inheritor of the Abrahamic blessing. The narrator tells us that the Jacob we see as he wakes up from this vision is not the arrogant young man assured of God's favor we have known but instead a human trembling with fear and awe that God is here with him, fifty-some miles out from his home—a significant distance in a world without cars. He now journeys far from familiar landscapes and peoples, seemingly on

4. In his translation of this passage Alter comments that the verb used for Jacob setting out is unusual because the verb used for Jacob going out on his journey in 29:1 is *nasa*, meaning "to lift" or "to carry." Alter writes: "Although eyes are frequently lifted or raised in these narratives, the idiom of lifting the feet occurs only here. . . . Perhaps this is a general idiom for beginning a particularly arduous journey on foot." Alter, *Five Books of Moses*, 152n1.

his own for many, many miles. We are told about this lengthy journey in a single verse. Maybe this is so not because the journey is unimportant but because even in the uneventful and dreary moments of Jacob's life we are given entry points to trek with him through an accelerated, but not omitted, journey from Bethel to the land of his uncle Laban. That is, the more rapidly paced narrative portions can function like the gaps we saw in the last chapter. This reminds me of how a movie will sometimes give us a short scene with a series of landscape vignettes depicting a long journey. These scenes often cover vast distances with a few strategic shots of a plane making its way through the clouds or figures running across mountain plains. The short glimpses invite us as viewers into these travels using only the briefest of screen time. Similarly, with the quickening pace over the many miles Jacob traveled, we might imagine his journey through worn trading routes that wind through the hill country of the Levant. Maybe we close our eyes and create our own picture of young Jacob setting out with a desolate and lonely landscape ahead of him.

Of course, not all rapidly narrated events, especially those as sparely rendered as this journey, offer the same richness as what we find here. By attending to the change in pacing in biblical stories, however, we will sometimes find that where the narrative speeds up, we are presented with the opportunity to slow down, to walk with Jacob on the dusty trade routes that take him far from his home and into unknown threat and possibility. Sometimes less is more.

In the stories of Abram's and Jacob's journeys (from and toward Haran respectively), these more rapidly paced narratives offer contrast in an evocative but not disruptive way within the broader pacing of the surrounding stories. But there are also stories where the pacing is so contrastive that it's unsettling. Recall the story of Nadab and Abihu's surprising and fiery end in Leviticus 10. In the prior chapter, I focused on the brevity with which the brothers' demise was narrated, but now let us zoom out a bit to take in the broader narrative that tells of the consecration of the first Aaronide priests.

Consider the standard narrated time of Leviticus 8–10. We enter a recognizable rhythm of instructions given and followed. First, God tells Moses to gather the assembly and do as he had been instructed regarding anointing and sacrifices (8:1–9). Moses does as directed in a narrative that unfolds his movements from gathering people at the tent of meeting to cleaning, dressing, and then anointing both the tent and the priests with oil (8:10–13). The narrative continues with the offerings being given just as God had instructed in the earlier chapters (8:14–29). Following these offerings, Aaron and his sons are anointed, consecrated, and given instructions to spend the next seven days at the entrance of the tent or else they will die (8:30–36). Unsurprisingly, the scene closes here and picks up again on the eighth day. Much like Moses's response to God's instructions, Aaron and his sons appear to respond with the same obedient action. In chapter 9 the proceedings of the eighth day continue this singsong quality with instructions given and followed (9:1–23). We are lulled (and possibly bored) into the steady pacing of this narrative.

As the eighth-day events culminate with the glory of the Lord appearing in fire (Lev. 9:24), however, the anticipated pace of instruction and obedient action is seriously disrupted: "Now Aaron's sons, Nadab and Abihu, each took his censer, put fire in it, and laid incense on it; and they offered unholy fire before the LORD, such as he had *not* commanded them" (10:1 NRSV). This abrupt act of disobedience contrasts sharply with the actions in the preceding chapters—not only because the pattern of instruction and obedient action is disrupted (no one gives instructions to Nadab and Abihu before they take their censers) but also because we have a sudden introduction of the word "not" (*lo*). In the preceding two chapters, we are told directly nine times that Moses and Aaron did as was commanded them. But, here, the calming pace of the narrative is disrupted because suddenly we have an outright act of disobedience. In fact, this act of disobedience (doing what is *not* commanded) shows up for the first time in the narrative of God instructing Moses beginning with details for building the tabernacle, which Moses scrupulously follows in the second half of Exodus. And, further, this judgment of doing what is *not* commanded shows up nowhere else in the chapters that follow.

This disruption continues in the next verse, where the disobedient action is immediately, seemingly instantaneously, followed by judgment: "And fire came out from the presence of the LORD and consumed them, and they died before the LORD" (Lev. 10:2 NRSV). In terms of pacing, we are quickly brought back on track. This sharp and sudden disruption of the standard narrated time—marked by instruction and then execution—in this moment with Nadab and Abihu's strange fire slows the narrated time to a snail's pace for the briefest moment as we watch the reversal: their offering of strange fire results in their being consumed by fire. Following a brief explanation in Leviticus 9:3, we return to the steady action of instructions given and followed.

In this story, we see that pacing can not only be understood as the consistent speed by which a story is told but can possess a rhythmic quality. When a rhythm is disrupted, even if only for a couple verses, it can emphasize a particular event like this one. We should see those disruptions not simply as out of place or as signs of poor writing or editing but as artistic signals meant to engage us in both the startling narrative action and the offbeat quality of that action. The breaking of the expected rhythm poses an invitation akin in some way to breakaway improvisation in jazz.

Here we see how the rhythm of pacing affects interpretation. Recall Wolfgang Iser's description of readers possessing a wandering viewpoint where reading is an *event* and not simply an accumulation of information. As we read stories, we become entangled in them. This entanglement is what produces a meaningful interpretation. In high school, a good friend would pick me up each morning for school. She loved techno music, which is a kind of electronic music produced by a DJ with the help of drum machines, synthesizers, and other forms of electronic music production. Often, she would pull up to my house with the music shaking her little Toyota, and I would get into a car filled with an overwhelming sense of varied sounds, depth, and beats. The music would transform tempos through these moments of disjunctive sound where suddenly the main beat would recede into the background or stop altogether and be replaced by an ethereal pause. I could feel it in my bones when these shifts happened. Knowing nothing about the intricacies of this musical form, I couldn't help but notice that something important was taking place.

Our experience as readers functions kind of like my experience of techno in the little Toyota. My friend could pick up on all the nuances of the change; my less attuned ear could pick up on something happening, though not with any level of sophistication. When we read a story, we *experience* meaning, even if we are not attuned to all the artistry of its storytelling. We may not be readily aware that a biblical story has a normative pace, but we likely take some note of it when we skip over an important event, slow down with a genealogy or narrative comment, or find that the rhythm of the story is disrupted (e.g., obedience, obedience, obedience, *dis*obedience). As readerly "ears" become more figuratively attuned to the artistry of storytelling through pacing, we can wander more deeply into the text. We can begin to "hear" the play of pacing as a way to wonder more deeply about these stories, inhabit the narrative worlds more profoundly, and maybe see ourselves more frequently in them.

What I hope for us to see in this overview of pacing is that a narrative diverging from its standard narrated time serves as more than artistic flourish. In biblical Hebrew narrative, some of the pacing cues are gilded over in translation, but pacing can serve as a helpful interpretive tool once you know it is there (even if you are reading in translation!). Pacing functions as an invitation to attend to disruptions of the regular rhythm of a story and consider how they shape our understanding of the narrative and its theology.

The *Waw* and the *Wayyiqtol* in the First Five Books

In many ways, the stories of the Pentateuch are not all that different from our own. Conjunctions are used to link clauses together and weave them into stories. In biblical Hebrew, the most common conjunction is a single letter, *waw* (pronounce the "w" here as a "v"). The *waw* can function like "and" in English, simply linking two words; it can offer contrast akin to "but," "or," and "nor"; it can show a temporal connection or focus like "then" or "now"; and it can communicate the causation of "so" or "because." Essentially one word (one letter!) translated most generically as "and" can signify a broad range of meanings within a narrative. The translator, as a reader of the text, must discern the specific meaning in context.

During my first year of biblical Hebrew, as I began to translate simple passages of Scripture, I remember realizing how many of the stories were both sparser and more cryptic than what I had grown accustomed to reading in translations. The stories as I knew them were not *wrong*, but I hadn't realized how much opportunity for variation there was in the translation from Hebrew to English. Ingenuity is always involved in translation, as the translator(s) must decide which words and phrases best capture in one language what is being said in another. Translation itself is an act of interpretation. But in biblical Hebrew, unlike the German I (barely) learned in high school, the work goes deeper than what is always there in translation. The rules of the game are different—or at least more complex—for translating Hebrew than for translating languages that share a more common heritage with English, such as German, Spanish, or French. The goal of learning biblical Hebrew was to be able to translate the Word of God, not Grimm's fairy tales or *Les Misérables*. The stakes felt much higher.

For me, one of the most distinctive challenges was in the range of the *waw* conjunction. Where I expected a contrasting conjunction, I found a *waw*. Where I encountered a list of rather monotonous instructions on building the tabernacle in the second half of Exodus, I found the *waw*. Where I expected the narrative to stop and the scene to shift, I found a *waw*. Though varied in its interpretive possibilities, the *waw* is not ambiguous in its function: it is the glue that holds stories, lists, and instructions together. I do not wish to suggest that the *waw* problematizes any assured translation. Nevertheless, there is a range of meaning in the *waw* that stands at the heart of the invitation I find in reading the Pentateuch closely and carefully. I hope that knowing the variability of a simple *waw* demonstrates how the invitation for the readers of these ancient stories is baked into them.

Think of the *waw* like a prefix or even a LEGO piece. It does not stand alone but latches onto the next word to link one clause to another. In Pentateuchal narrative, the two most common ways we see the *waw* at work are as a disjunctive *waw*, when it is attached to something other than a verb, and the *wayyiqtol* form (the *wa-* is the *waw*), when it is attached to a verb form (see fig. 3.1).

Figure 3.1

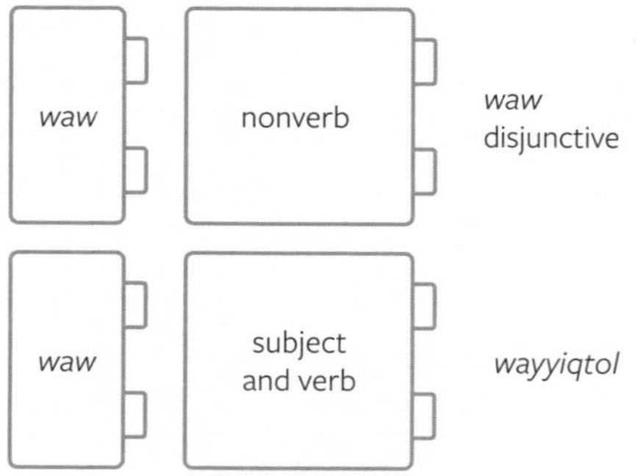

The Waw Disjunctive

The disjunctive *waw* shows up less frequently than the *wayyiqtol*. Its disjunctive quality alerts the reader to a change either in scene or setting or in the action of the characters.[5] We can see the disjunctive *waw* (represented in my translations that follow as *and*) alerting us to a change of scene in Numbers 11:31, when the narrative shifts. Moses ends his conversation with Joshua and returns to camp as God sends a wind from the sea to bring quail to the wilderness wanderers. "And a young man ran and told Moses, 'Eldad and Medad are prophesying in the camp.' And Joshua son of Nun, the assistant of Moses, one of his chosen men, said, 'My lord Moses, stop them!' But Moses said to him, 'Are you jealous for my sake? Would that all the LORD's people were prophets, and that the LORD would put his spirit on them!' And Moses and the elders of Israel returned to the camp" (Num. 11:27–30 NRSV).

Following this narrative, as the elders return to camp, we read: "*And* a wind went out from the LORD" (Num. 11:31). In many translations, including the NRSV, a section break appears between verses 30 and 31, alerting readers to the change in setting. The story here shifts our eyes from the mountain to the sea, as it also shifts from the realm of human to the realm of divine. Conversely, with a dramatic change in action in Numbers 12, we can see the *waw* function to emphasize or focus on a particular scene. Here God responds directly to Miriam and Aaron's complaints about the new wife Moses has taken: "*And* the cloud departed from above the tent and look, Miriam leprous like snow" (12:10). Much like the sun peeking out from behind a cloud to paint the landscape with vibrant light, here the *waw* disjunctive functions to draw attention immediately to Miriam's implausible transformation.

As we encounter the *waw* disjunctive, often signaled by "when" or "then" in English translation, we are left to wonder what the narrator might have had in mind in this shift in place or point of view. What aspect of the story is opened up with these shifts? Do they communicate something theologically? Especially consider when the narrator shifts from the actions of the people to the workings of God. How might this back-and-forth open up interpretive possibilities for us as readers?

5. Waltke and O'Connor, *Introduction to Biblical Hebrew Syntax*, 650–52.

The Wayyiqtol

The most common form of linking clauses in biblical Hebrew narrative is found in the *wayyiqtol*.[6] The vast majority of stories you will read in the Pentateuch will rely solely on the *wayyiqtol* not only to draw together a key scene but to connect broader portions of narrative. One of the greatest invitations we find in biblical Hebrew narrative is in the way the *wayyiqtol* uniquely functions in Hebrew narrative.

My simple retelling of *The Hobbit* demonstrates how this term works in Hebrew narrative: "AND Gandalf visited AND many dwarves joined him AND Bilbo journeyed far from the Shire AND he saw trolls AND he found a ring AND he told no one what he found AND he traveled to the Lonely Mountain AND he met a dragon AND he returned home." Notice how the use of "and" connects the clauses without using subordinate clauses that elaborate on these basic actions. The *wayyiqtol* form functions like "and" in this example, while also functioning as a punctuation mark in our translated texts (biblical Hebrew narrative does not separate clauses with punctuation marks like we have in English and other modern languages). Readers must infer causal connections because the text itself does not provide them. For example, there is no obvious hint in my summary above that the key moment for Bilbo was not dwarves or dragons or far travels but the secret of possessing the ring. The pacing of this clipped version of *The Hobbit* doesn't give us much opportunity to fill in gaps or give us a sense of how these flat descriptions relate to one another and the broader story. The function of "and" sets a clipped pace for standard narration focused primarily on action rather than subordinate clauses that unpack the events. Here, we see the way the use of the *wayyiqtol* produces the spare and punchy style of biblical Hebrew narrative that keeps readers concentrated on the events themselves.

The *wayyiqtol* not only offers a spare style of narration but impacts the pacing of a narrative. Through the repetitive "and," a series of actions unfold without language to soften, explain, or distinguish between actions: "AND this AND this AND this . . ." A biblical example can help you see how this works in the Pentateuch. Consider the well-known story of Moses encountering the burning bush in Exodus 3. After God's messenger

6. In his Hebrew grammar textbook, Travis West defines the *wayyiqtol* as "the peculiar storytelling verb 'tense' in Hebrew. . . . It is used overwhelmingly by the narrators of biblical stories." West, *Biblical Hebrew*, 390.

appears to him in the burning-but-not-burnt bush, Moses takes a closer look at the odd sight. The Lord then calls to Moses in Exodus 3:4. Here are a few of the more well-known translations of this verse:

> When the Lord saw that he turned aside to see, God called to him out of the bush, "Moses! Moses!" And he said, "Here I am." (ESV)

> When the Lord saw that he had gone over to look, God called to him from within the bush, "Moses! Moses!" And Moses said, "Here I am." (NIV)

> When the Lord saw that he had turned aside to see, God called to him out of the bush, "Moses, Moses!" And he said, "Here I am." (NRSV)

Compare these to my translation of the verse with the *wayyiqtol* reflected through "*AND*":

> AND the Lord saw that he turned aside to see
> AND God called to him from out of the bush
> AND he said, "Moses, Moses."
> AND he said, "Here I am."

The well-known translations do a fantastic job of conveying what is happening in this verse. I do not wish to diminish the usefulness of these translations or insist that you master Hebrew to truly understand what is going on in the text. Instead, I want you to notice what is not so easily seen in the common Bible translations: how the *wayyiqtol* sets a rhythm for the unfolding of the story. The use of "when" to suggest a temporal marker in preparation for God's call to Moses offers us a smoother read, but it also veils one of the distinctive drumbeats of biblical Hebrew narrative. The *wayyiqtol* establishes a rhythm within a narrative scene guided by action and dialogue. The clipped pace of these biblical stories emphasizes their spare quality and can deceptively make it seem as though these stories are simple or easy.

Let's return to Genesis 12:10–16 as Abram and Sarai journey to Egypt, with the *wayyiqtol* as "AND" (and the disjunctive *waw* in italic):

> 10AND there was a famine in the land
> AND Abram went down toward Egypt

[11]AND he neared Egypt
AND he said to Sarai: "Look, I know that you are a beautiful woman [12]and
when the Egyptians see you and they will say, 'This is his woman and they
will kill me and let you live.' [13]Say to them that you are my sister so that
it will go well with me because of you and so that I will remain alive for
your sake."
[14]AND when Abram entered Egypt
AND the Egyptians saw the woman that she was very beautiful.
[15]AND when Pharaoh's commanders saw
AND they praised her to Pharaoh
AND the woman was taken into Pharaoh's house
[16]*and* concerning Abram, he was made happy for her sake
AND there were [given] to him sheep and cattle and male donkeys and male
servants and female servants and female donkeys and camels.

In the next verse, we are given the judgment of God upon the pharaoh's head, but we are left without any overt moral judgment of Abram and no insight into Sarai's experience of the events.

While the moral judgments we make in this story are a worthy investigation, what I want to notice here is the pacing of the narrative and what it does to us as readers who are seeking to understand the story. We plod along: there is a famine, so Abram journeys toward Egypt, and as he and Sarai get close to Egypt, he offers an extended rationale for why they should deceive the Egyptians. After his closing words to Sarai, we come under the gaze of the Egyptians, but we don't hear a word from Sarai. Later, after Sarai is brought into Pharaoh's house, we are left with Abram. We do not know how much time passed between Sarai's departure and Abram's bounty or the amount of time between the events in verse 16 and God's judgment that follows. At face value, the story unfolds in a steady and straightforward manner. But the pace itself works as a kind of deception, keeping the less perceptive reader from attending to the questions that remain not only of things unsaid but of the harmony or incongruity between the clock time and narrative time while Sarai dwelled in Pharaoh's house.

Of course, the narrator could have simply told us that Abram was faithful in this deception to the broader mission God had given him, and so it was worth the risk to Sarai. Or the narrator could have told us that Sarai herself gave Abram this idea, knowing that she could use her beauty to assure both her and Abram's overall safety. Or the narrator could have mentioned that Sarai was in fact safe the entire time she was in Pharaoh's house. Or that she exited Pharaoh's chambers with tears and anger in her eyes. The fact that we are *not* told and are instead given just enough information to know that Sarai was for some time not with Abram and instead in the home of a powerful stranger invites us to wonder at the interpersonal dynamics and details of her time away. Had we been told, "Oh, don't worry, reader, Sarai was protected from any harm the entire time she was in Pharaoh's company," we likely would feel less inclined to wonder at the unfolding of events, satisfied that we know what we need to know about the story. And, of course, the effect would be the same if the narrator had given us an explicit description of untoward events while Sarai resided in Pharaoh's home. The story's pace does not slow down or pause here for the narrator to comment; instead, as the story plods on, we are given just enough to be invested in wandering and wondering through the details of the narrative we are given.

As a final example, recall the story of Jacob setting out from Bethel at the start of Genesis 29. Compare the familiar NRSV translation to my own, where I more overtly render the *wayyiqtol* ("AND") and *waw* disjunctive ("*and*") in Genesis 29:1–2:

> [1]Then Jacob went on his journey, and came to the land of the people of
> the east. [2]As he looked, he saw a well in the field and three flocks of sheep
> lying there beside it. (NRSV)

> [1]AND Jacob went on his journey
> AND he went to the land of the people of the east
> [2]AND he saw
> *and* behold a well in the field
> *and* behold three flocks of sheep lying beside it. (my trans.)

There is nothing inherently wrong with the NRSV translation. The thing to notice here is that where a common English translation smooths over the Hebrew's transitions and repetitions, we find in my more clunky translation the rather gruff pacing of the narrative: "AND this AND this AND this." What I have said before bears repeating here: you do not need to know Hebrew to appreciate the sparely wrought and curtly paced narrative that frequently shows up in the Pentateuchal narratives. Simply knowing that these literary devices, especially that of the common *wayyiqtol*, stand behind our translations invites us more deeply into these crucial stories.

Next we will move to a close reading of a central biblical story to draw out how pacing impacts meaning. Before doing so, I want to offer one practical resource for those who want to access the spare quality of biblical Hebrew narrative more clearly without learning biblical Hebrew. Robert Alter has translated the Hebrew Bible in a way that is both fresh and attentive to features like the *wayyiqtol*. In his introduction, where he defends yet *another* English translation of the Hebrew Bible, he lays out his hope for this work: "The present translation is an experiment in re-presenting the Bible—and, above all, biblical narrative prose—in a language that conveys with some precision the semantic nuances and the lively orchestration of literary effects of the Hebrew and at the same time has stylistic and rhythmic integrity as literary English."[7] That is, he aims to make the distinctive Hebrew quality of the biblical storytelling present in his translation, while also making it enjoyable and readable in English. One of the key parts of this dual goal is to reflect the lack of subordinate clauses—the parataxis—present in biblical Hebrew narrative. Alter notes,

> Although there are certainly instances of significant syntactic subordination, the characteristic biblical syntax is additive, working with parallel clauses linked by "and"—which in the Hebrew is not even a separate word but rather a particle, *waw* (it means "hook"), that is prefixed to the first word of the clause.
>
> The assumption of most modern translators has been that this sort of syntax will be either unintelligible or at least alienating to the modern readers, and so should be entirely rearranged as modern English. . . . It ignores the fact that *parataxis is the essential literary vehicle of biblical narrative*: it is the way the ancient Hebrew writers saw the world, linked events in it, artfully ordered it, and narrated it, and one gets a very different world if their syntax is jettisoned.[8]

The parataxis present through the *wayyiqtol* plays a central role in the way a biblical story unfolds in the older testament. Alter aims to retain that

7. Alter, *Hebrew Bible*, 1:1.
8. Alter, *Hebrew Bible*, 1:xx.

distinctiveness while also making the English translation highly readable and beautiful in its own right.

Especially suited for our purposes, Alter's translation opts for the general "and" when rendering the *waw*, rather than any of a number of other English translations for this conjunction. While we should be wary of making one person's translation of the text the sole or central version we use—be it Alter's *The Hebrew Bible* or Eugene Peterson's *The Message*—there is benefit to supplementing the translations made by communities of scholars with these more singularly focused offerings. Alter's translation serves as a helpful supplement when we are reading to be more attentive to the pacing of the "AND this AND this AND this" of biblical Hebrew narrative.

Case Study: Genesis 32:22–32

Arguably the story par excellence to see biblical Hebrew narrative at work in the Pentateuch is found in the account of the wrestling-match-turned-blessing on the banks of the Jabbok River in Genesis 32. Recently departed from his uncle Laban in the north on rather tense terms, Jacob now faces south and prepares for what is potentially an even more hostile confrontation with his brother, Esau, from whom he had taken both birthright and blessing. This story in Genesis 32 serves a key role in the broader unfolding of the Abrahamic promise in the early story of ancient Israel. Jacob takes on a new name—like Abraham before him and the apostle Paul much later—to signal a new thing that God is doing both in his lifetime and for future generations. This story also serves as one of my personal favorite stories in the whole of Scripture for its evocative quality and the reminder that God's blessing sometimes comes through pain that results in a kind of limp.

The function of the *wayyiqtol* in this story exemplifies the interpretive richness available to readers. The *wayyiqtol* creates a rather unsettling effect when compared to the standard contemporary translations of the story. The story itself unfolds before the reader without much in the way of explanation. To draw out the dramatic effect of the *wayyiqtol*, I will break the story into four parts: preparation (vv. 22–23), wrestling (vv. 24–25), questioning and blessing (vv. 26–29), and resolution (vv. 30–32). Each part begins with a side-by-side comparison of the NRSV (a well-respected contemporary translation) and my own translation, with the *wayyiqtol* indicated by "AND."

Preparation (vv. 22–23)

> [22]The same night he got up and took his two wives, his two maids, and his eleven children, and crossed the ford of the Jabbok. [23]He took them and sent them across the stream, and likewise everything that he had. (NRSV)

> [22]AND he arose that same night
> AND he took his two wives and his two handmaids and his eleven children
> AND he crossed over the ford of Jabbok.
> [23]AND he took them
> AND he brought them across the brook
> AND he brought across all that was his. (my trans.)

Jacob has just executed all his big-picture plans for the forthcoming strained reunion with his brother. He directed his servants to bring wave upon wave of livestock to pass into Esau's land, with each successive arrival declaring both Jacob's prosperity and the extent of gifts that he brings for his brother. Now, he looks to those people and items that remain with him, which are his most valued people (and likely his most valued possessions). He gathers everyone together and brings them and all he owns across the Jabbok at the river crossing.

Here, we can see the particular way that the *wayyiqtol* paces the narrative. In both the NRSV and in my translation, these two verses are dense with verbs. Jacob arises, takes, crosses, takes again, and sends. The spirit of the two translations is the same, but in my translation you can more greatly sense the urgency of these actions: "AND he arose . . . AND he took . . . AND he crossed . . . AND he took . . . AND he brought . . . AND he brought." In taking note of the effect of the *wayyiqtol* here, we might see this literary device function as a kind of stage direction in a play.[9] We can imagine Jacob moving with anxious energy as he gathers and sends all that most matters to him across the river. The pacing picks up, signaling that the story is moving toward a significant moment. After all his preparations earlier in the chapter, here we draw near to a key moment for Jacob—though not likely what he (or we) expected.

J. P. Fokkelman reflects on the brevity of key stories in the Old Testament, noting that "some of the profoundest and most exciting stories are

9. With gratitude to Anna Beaudry, who illuminated this stage-direction effect of the *wayyiqtol*.

remarkably short but are found close to a long text which moves at a very relaxed pace."[10] We find an example of this shift in pacing here in the narrated events that lead up to these preparations at the river and what follows. In both the preceding and subsequent events, there is a much more relaxed standard narrated pacing. Like a foot pressing on the gas pedal, verses 22–23 bring action in rapid succession, preparing us for a dramatic change.[11]

Wrestling (vv. 24-25)

> 24Jacob was left alone; and a man wrestled with him until daybreak. 25When the man saw that he did not prevail against Jacob, he struck him on the hip socket; and Jacob's hip was put out of joint as he wrestled with him. (NRSV)

> 24AND Jacob remained by himself
> AND a man wrestled with him until daybreak.
> 25AND he saw that he was not able to prevail over him
> AND he struck his hip socket
> AND he dislocated Jacob's hip socket while wrestling him. (my trans.)

These two verses serve as one of the most memorable scenes in the book of Genesis, the broader Pentateuch, and arguably the Old Testament as a whole. Artistic depictions, hymns, and poetry pick up on this image of a man alone at night wrestling with God. After all the preparation, we are given the action of *the* central event in Jacob's life in the span of a couple verses. Continuing the idea of the *wayyiqtol* functioning as stage direction, here we are invited to see Jacob standing alone on the banks of the Jabbok—when suddenly, seemingly from the shadows, comes a man. We don't know who this man is, and presumably we share that lack of recognition with Jacob in the moment. We are given very little in terms

10. Fokkelman, "Genesis," 39.

11. Before the story of his wrestling match, Jacob makes detailed preparations for meeting his estranged brother. These preparations include precise instructions to his servants, through whom Jacob hopes the giving of gifts and assuring words will soften the exchange when Esau finally encounters Jacob (Gen. 32:3–5, 13–21). In addition to these preparations, the narrative also includes Jacob's prayer to God recounting God's promises to Jacob and a plea for deliverance (32:9–12). Following the wrestling account, Esau and Jacob reunite via Esau's initial approach (33:1–3); Esau's enthusiastic response to the meeting (33:4–7); and Jacob's insistence that Esau receive his gifts (33:8–14).

of imagining this wrangling, only that they wrestle until dawn begins to break.

To add to the spare quality of verse 24, we find in the next verse a dizzying back-and-forth, where discerning which "he" is which disorients readers because the narrative rapidly shifts from one subject to another. The NRSV resolves this tension by inserting designations in the first part of verse 25 to make clear which "he" was Jacob and which was the unknown "man." We find similar interpretive smoothing in a number of other common translations:

> When the man saw that he could not defeat him, he struck Jacob's hip socket as they wrestled and dislocated his hip. (CSB)

> When the man saw that he could not overpower him, he touched the socket of Jacob's hip so that his hip was wrenched as he wrestled with the man. (NIV)

> When the man saw that he would not win the match, he touched Jacob's hip and wrenched it out of its socket. (NLT)

Of note, the NKJV retains the effect of the *wayyiqtol* but capitalizes references to one of the actors to resolve any confusion: "Now when He saw that He did not prevail against him, He touched the socket of his hip; and the socket of Jacob's hip was out of joint as He wrestled with him." These translations go out of their way to resolve what I am identifying as the dizzying effect of this verse—a dizzying effect that is perhaps part of its message. We are reading a story about a late-night encounter with a mysterious figure whom Jacob later identifies as God, one that ends with a wounding blessing that reorients the rest of Jacob's, now Israel's, life.

Of course, the end of verse 25 clarifies that it was Jacob's hip put out of socket. But what I want us to notice is that it takes three successive *wayyiqtol* forms to get to that clarification: (1) "AND he saw," (2) "AND he struck," (3) "AND he dislocated." It is not until we get midway through this third clause that it's clear who strikes and who is struck. This example is a hard one to identify in translation, though we do get a hint of it in the KJV, and it's even more pronounced in Alter's translation: "AND he saw that he had not won out against him AND he touched his hip-socket AND Jacob's hip-socket was wrenched as he wrestled with him."[12]

Walter Brueggemann reflects on this story by noting that "clearly, this is no ordinary story." The incident is shrouded in darkness, with man and (divine?) man wrestling all night, a match that ends in both wounding and blessing.[13] Might there be some value to recognizing that sometimes we are invited into the experience of an unfolding event and not solely an explanation of what happened? The use of the *wayyiqtol* to disorient through a rapidly paced description of the back-and-forth in the dark of night enriches the invitation of this extraordinary story inviting us to make out the silhouettes of these two figures wrestling all night on the banks of the Jabbok.

These semiopaque stories offer not only a description of the style of biblical Hebrew storytelling but a hint at what these stories are *for*. If stories like this one are simply to convey that Jacob was a man blessed by God or to explain a new name, we could just as easily have received that through line without the syntactically cryptic storytelling. If we are meant simply to understand this story as an analogy to our own "wrestling" with God in dark nights of the soul (or something of that sort), maybe the story could have offered us something more explicit about *why* the wrestling occurred and, even more, why such a permanent kind of wounding occurred. Of course, this story does offer us all of the above, but there seems to be more here than straightforward textbook information about Jacob's life or allegory of contemplation for the modern reader. We are invited to enjoy, to imagine, and to engage with these stories in ways that spark our imaginations, frustrate our assurances of having them entirely figured out, and (hopefully) keep us coming back to find new or renewed observations.

Questioning and Blessing (vv. 26–29)

[26]Then he said, "Let me go, for the day is breaking." But Jacob said, "I will not let you go, unless you bless me." [27]So he said to him, "What is your name?" And he said, "Jacob." [28]Then the man said, "You shall no longer be called Jacob, but Israel, for you have striven with God and with humans, and have prevailed." [29]Then Jacob asked him, "Please tell me your name." But he said, "Why is it that you ask my name?" And there he blessed him. (NRSV)

12. Alter, *Hebrew Bible*, 1:121 (capitalization added to reflect the three-part movement of this verse through the *wayyiqtol*).

13. Brueggemann, *Genesis*, 267.

> [26]AND he said: "Please, let me go, for the dawn ascends."
> AND he said: "I will not let you go unless you bless me."
> [27]AND he said to him: "What is your name?"
> AND he said: "Jacob."
> [28]AND he said: "Jacob is no longer your name, but rather 'Israel,' for you contended with God and with men and you prevailed."
> [29]AND Jacob questioned
> AND he said: "Please, tell me your name."
> AND he said: "Why is it that you ask for my name?"
> AND he blessed him there. (my trans.)

We continue some of the dizzying effect of identifying subjects in verses 26–27 with five consecutive "AND he said" clauses, but this time it's easier to identify the subject, both with the request for a blessing, as Jacob very recently asked God directly for help and deliverance early in this chapter, and with the clear identifier, as Jacob gives his name. In tandem with the opaque quality of the slowing narration, we also have a slowing down of pace as the story returns more to the standard narrated time of the early narrative. The dialogue slows and focuses on the scene, making clock time and narrated time parallel, which is particularly noticeable if this dialogue portion is read aloud. Here we do not have stage directions but a script that helps us imagine these two figures—both likely glistening with sweat, one likely in quite a bit of pain—in conversation as the sun rises.

The narrative itself matches well what we have come to know about Jacob from earlier stories. He is clever and driven, and he sees an opportunity as he presses the man for a blessing and then for his name. The man grants him one of these requests but not the other. In a wonderful way, the pacing of these verses functions much like catching one's breath after a sprint. The dialogue slows and focuses us as readers, and Jacob as narrative agent, to assess what just happened. What I most appreciate about attending to the *wayyiqtol* in this narrative is what is absent. In the NRSV, we find a dialogue that leads us through the engagement: "*Then* he said . . . *But* Jacob said . . . *So* he said . . . *And* he said . . . *Then* the man said . . . *Then* Jacob asked . . . *But* he said . . . *And* there he blessed . . ." I add the italics here to show how the *wayyiqtol* with its nondescript function of connecting clauses is given interpretive flourish to offer a less clunky and more seamless translation of the dialogue. Once again, I am not saying there is anything wrong or unseemly in this translation choice. Instead, I simply want us to recognize that the opaque quality and readerly invitation is more readily apparent when we can identify all these conjunctions as *choices* made to help us as readers along.

For me, seeing the "and" here translated more generically, particularly in verse 29 when Jacob seeks the man's name, draws out the disorienting effect of the narrative. Jacob tries to get a handle on the situation, tries to bring to light what exactly just happened by questioning and asking after this wrestler's name. This is harder to see in the NRSV. There the wrestler answers Jacob contrastively, with "But he said, 'Why is it that you ask my name?'" With the nondescript "AND" of the *wayyiqtol*, we might see that the wrestler isn't refusing an answer so much as giving one rhetorically: Why is it that you ask my name, Jacob? *You know who I am.*

Resolution (vv. 30–32)

> 30 So Jacob called the place Peniel, saying, "For I have seen God face to face, and yet my life is preserved." 31 The sun rose upon him as he passed Penuel, limping because of his hip. 32 Therefore to this day the Israelites do not eat the thigh muscle that is on the hip socket, because he struck Jacob on the hip socket at the thigh muscle. (NRSV)

> 30 AND Jacob declared: "The name of this place is 'Peniel,' for I saw God face to face,
> AND yet my life is spared."
> 31 AND the sun arose before him just as he left Penuel,
> AND he was limping because of his hip. 32 Because of this, the Israelites do not eat sinew of the hip, which is on the socket of the leg, until this day, for he struck the hip socket of Jacob in the sinew of the thigh. (my trans.)

Rather stunningly, following the blessing, we are left alone once again with Jacob. In the resolution that follows, the wrestler/angel-man is nowhere to be found. The *wayyiqtol* forcibly continues the story from blessing to Jacob's declaration without any stage exit for the wrestler. Where did he go? Did he walk away into the sunrise, fading like a mirage into the golden light of daybreak? Or did he vanish like an apparition before Jacob's tired eyes? The story moves along, first to Jacob's reflection of the event and then to the narrator's note without so much as a nod to the other man's departure. Here the pacing is strange, as it both glosses over any exit of one actor and slows to a standstill with the narrator's comment in verse 32, pulling us as readers out of the scene.

Conclusion

Genesis 32:22–32 helps us to see the ways that the pacing of a narrative through the use of the *wayyiqtol* invites us more deeply into the narrative. Sometimes, the *wayyiqtol* offers a kind of stage direction, helping us to imagine the sequence of events unfolding as anticipation grows. Other times, the *wayyiqtol* unfolds events in such rapid succession, adding both excitement and complexity to a scene, that we must pause to catch our breath. The *wayyiqtol* also provides a drumbeat to a story—*and* this *and* this *and* this—that can offer us crucial moments in a flash and skip over others without missing a beat. Knowing this literary feature is at work, even when reading in translation, opens up a new depth of meaning in even such a familiar story as Jacob wrestling at Peniel.

Both in slowing down and in racing forward, pacing plays a crucial role in our experience as readers. Attention to these changes invites us to engage more richly with stories generally, and this may be particularly true for the most familiar Bible stories. As we read the stories of the Pentateuch, attention to the distinctive quality of biblical Hebrew storytelling opens up new opportunities to wonder and wander as we read. Notably, the generic quality of the *wayyiqtol* helps us to see the distinctive brevity of Hebrew narrative, which uses a seemingly steady succession of independent clauses to shift the pacing of a story as we read.

The invitation found in paying attention to narrative pacing unveils possibilities not only in the narrative world but in our own imaginations. It gives us the chance to wonder how God works in the world. When we are confronted by God, is it like Jacob's experience, reflected in the narrative pacing, which disorients and requires wrangling and questioning to discern God's presence in our midst? Does the absence of certain narrative details, skipped over by an increased narrative pace, force us as readers to slow down and wonder what else we might be skipping over in our hurry to get to the next thing? Might we find an invitation not only to wonder and wander but to contemplate the deep mysteries of faith in what is unsaid or only offered via allusion?

CHAPTER 4

Characterization

Introduction

Have you ever read a novel where you felt like you truly *knew* a character? Or watched a show where a character was too glib, jolly, or shallow to be believable? The way a storyteller crafts a character makes all the difference for a story's overall quality. One of my favorite authors, the Southern gothic novelist and short-story writer Flannery O'Connor, has a knack for riding the line between the bizarre and the believable in her protagonists. O'Connor makes even the most freakish of characters somehow relatable and the most despicable lovable. She is able to pull off such a feat because she has mastered the craft of characterization, knowing which literary strokes will paint a protagonist (or villain) that readers find credible.

We come to know characters through different tools of characterization. Sometimes, like in the novel *Jane Eyre*, an author uses a "more is more" approach. Charlotte Brontë offers readers all kinds of information to help them know her main character, Jane; most notably, Brontë allows Jane to directly address readers, which illuminates her internal turmoil and emotions. Conversely, O'Connor, in her story "A Good Man Is Hard to Find," uses a "less is more" approach to help us get to know the grandmother (in fact, the grandmother isn't even given a name!). There is no one right way to portray a figure in a story. What is important is that however a character is rendered—"more is more," "less is more," or somewhere in between—the character must be believable as an agent in the story. It's highly likely that your favorite stories are your favorites precisely for the author's skill in characterization.

The stories in the Pentateuch are filled with memorable characters who defined the identity of ancient Israel. Many central figures—including Adam and Eve; Abraham, Sarah, and Hagar; Joseph; Moses, Aaron, and Miriam; and young Joshua—are brought to life through a more O'Connoresque approach where "less is more" in terms of characterization. This invites us as readers to get involved and to get to know these central characters through our imaginations more than we would through a simple, direct textual description of them and their thoughts.

Our case study in the second half of this chapter is one of the most enigmatic of all those we will explore in the Pentateuch: the characterization of the God of Abraham, Isaac, and Jacob. While some of the modes of characterization of God are rather typical, we also find the strangest sorts of descriptions used to capture the challenge of speaking about God at work in the world. The paradoxical quality of some of these characterizations—God in burning bushes that do not burn, God suddenly deciding to kill a chosen prophet, and God communing with Moses in the strangest of clouds—signals a special kind of figure in the narratives, one who cannot be captured in the same way other characters can. Learning to pay attention to how the biblical storytellers present their characters not only helps us hear those stories better; it also helps us recognize when something different is happening. The characterization of God articulates an important theological distinction: God is not simply another character in this cast. Instead, we as readers discover a figure of a different sort.

Direct and Indirect Characterization

The Dictionary of Narratology defines characterization as "the set of techniques resulting in the constitution of character. Characterization can be more or less direct."[1] A more direct characterization includes physical description (e.g., short, tall, gaunt, rotund, beautiful, ugly), temperament (e.g., kind, generous, vindictive, angry), and inner emotions (e.g., fearful, ashamed, jealous, smitten, hopeful). These descriptions can be provided by a narrator or through the eyes of another character via their dialogue,

1. Prince, *Dictionary of Narratology*, 13.

insight, or attitude. Less direct characterization comes by way of inferring traits about a character from only their action or speech. As an example of indirect acts of characterization in real life, you can learn a lot about a person by watching how they respond to a stressful situation like, say, overhearing a conversation with a waiter when an order does not meet expectations. We make judgments about people all the time through indirect means, so it is unsurprising that we are given the same opportunities to get to know characters within a story in this same sort of indirect way.

Indirect characterization serves as the predominant means of characterization in biblical Hebrew narrative. As Shimon Bar-Efrat helpfully summarizes, "It is in the nature of the indirect method that characters are not defined comprehensively, but that their personalities emerge gradually from the totality of their appearances and actions during the course of the narrative. The indirect approach cannot make it clear to us at the outset of the narrative what the character's nature is, and this will not be evident until the end, when we are able to review and combine all the relevant facts."[2] Importantly, Bar-Efrat highlights that to come to know a character primarily through indirect characterization means that you will construct a picture of a character as you read and only come to make an assessment of who they are when all is said and done. Sometimes, this comprehensive assessment spans only a handful of chapters of a biblical book (like the story of Hagar in Gen. 16–21), and other times it spans multiple books (like the story of Moses in Exodus, Leviticus, Numbers, and Deuteronomy).

The oblique characterization cues biblical Hebrew narratives offer us are also sparse. Remember, one of the defining characteristics of ancient Israel's stories is their brevity. We are often given very little from which to infer very much. This overall spare style of storytelling results in indirect characterization that demands much from readers. We have to work hard at understanding what is going on in a story and how we are supposed to respond. We are given limited opportunities to pick up on the kind of character we are dealing with in a given story. Sometimes, like we saw in the story of Nadab and Abihu, we are given the very slightest of hints on which to judge whether the character has had a moral failing or demonstrated exemplary obedience.

2. Bar-Efrat, *Narrative Art in the Bible*, 89.

The limited material for building up our picture of a character in a biblical story means that we sometimes can find different understandings of the same figure across time and place. Those most readily identified as heroes may appear villainous when read by the oppressed; the figures traditionally overlooked may be drawn out with surprising dynamism by marginalized readers. Abraham, the great friend of God, also asks his wife to lie to protect him and mistreats an enslaved woman under his care. Jacob, the one who wrestles with God, also deceives, connives, and misleads in making a name for himself. Jesus also teaches us in the Gospels about the power of discerning the quality of a character with spare information through his use of parables and his call for those with ears to hear and with eyes to see. The parables, like the stories of the Old Testament, require work on the part of readers to make judgments, not only about the moral of a story but also about who is deemed a hero or a fool.

One of the more interesting literary devices employed for indirect characterization in biblical Hebrew narrative is the formula of command/fulfillment where we come to know about a character through their obedience or disobedience to a command, most often one given by God or by one of God's messengers. This formula is familiar to us, as we likely use it every day: I praise my dog as "a good girl" when I tell her to "wait" as I pour kibble into her dog bowl and she patiently obeys; and I, in the role of professor, reward a student with a high grade when they adhere to the syllabus's assignment instructions. In biblical narrative, we find a similar function when God gives commands. We do not frequently see God directly praise someone, like I would an obedient dog or a successful student. Instead, we are left to deduce a judgment about the character from the extent to which a command was fulfilled. This discernment involves closely reading the story before us and understanding the broader narrative and theology present in the biblical text. Indirect characterization requires work on our part as readers to make a judgment about a character based on their action (or inaction).

The first example of this formula comes in the early pages of Genesis with Adam and Eve in the garden. In this familiar story, God tells the first humans that all fruit of the garden is available for food, except they must not eat from the tree of the knowledge of good and evil: "You may freely eat of every tree of the garden; but of the tree of the knowledge of good and evil you shall not eat, for in the day that you eat of it you shall die"

(Gen. 2:16–17 NRSV). In the next chapter, with the riches of the garden on full display, the serpent tempts Adam and Eve with the one prohibited tree, asking Eve, "Did God say, 'You shall not eat from any tree in the garden'?" (3:1 NRSV). Eve responds, clarifying that they "may eat of the fruit of the trees in the garden; but *God said*, 'You shall not eat of the fruit of the tree that is in the middle of the garden.'" So far, so good. But Eve then continues: "*Nor shall you touch it*, or you shall die" (3:2–3 NRSV). Of course, this interaction between Eve and the serpent can be read many ways, as the history of tradition has done both more and (mostly) less generously toward Eve. But my purpose in pointing to this passage here is not to belittle or blame Eve but rather to show the very human response that we see throughout biblical narrative and in broader human history—the response of negotiating between what we have been told and how we act on those instructions. This response can be something consciously or unconsciously done, well-intentioned or not.

God said nothing about touching the tree. Yet Eve makes a point not only to answer the serpent's question but to reiterate in her response that "God said . . ." both what God *did* say earlier and the addendum about touching the tree. Quite possibly, this addition is simply Eve's own interpretation of the force of God's command, especially as it comes by way of Adam's instruction to her. (Remember, Eve was not the one given the initial command.) Significantly, rather than laying blame, the flourish added to the command functions narratively to prepare us for the events that follow. Here the story foreshadows the radical act of disobedience to come, by both Eve and Adam. Importantly for our purposes here, notice the incongruity between God's instructions and Eve's response in word, then later her and Adam's response in deed in the eating of the fruit.

In this archetypal story of disobedience we find this tool of characterization creating a disharmony between a command and the fulfillment of that command. Through the discrepancy between what God *did* say in Genesis 2 and what God was *reported* as saying in Genesis 3, we readers receive a hint that Eve (and Adam, her accomplice who is present but does not correct her addition) is vulnerable to disobedience well before any fruit is plucked from the tree. Divine instructions are not being followed exactly, even in the dialogue—though again, the cause of the discrepancy is not clear. We don't know Adam's or Eve's inner thoughts or motivations. The serpent here functions helpfully to attune readers to exactly what is going on in the unspoken aspects of the scene.

I wonder about the serpent's true intentions in asking Eve to recall the instructions she received from God. Perhaps the serpent was not simply tempting her to disobey but was gaining a better picture of these two moral agents standing before him. That is, maybe the serpent was measuring the moral fortitude of Eve and Adam by going about the conversation in the way he did.[3] Who knows? Had Eve answered the serpent with God's verbatim instructions, maybe the serpent would have known he did not have such an easy target for temptation. Of course, this reading is speculative, but speculation is part of the joy of reading biblical narrative. If nothing else, I hope that attending to the discrepancy between God's command and Eve's report of it helps us delve more deeply into this story, expanding our interpretive view and adding dimension to Eve, the serpent, and even Adam in this narrative. I hope we see how the artistic invitation through characterization draws us more deeply into even the most familiar of Bible stories.

In the many biblical stories that follow this early one, we find again and again that we learn about the quality of a character in terms of whether they act in harmony or in disharmony with God's instructions. This original story of disobedience speaks not only of the theological nature of humans before God but also narratively of the ways that we can learn about a character indirectly. Arguably, the definitive action of Adam and Eve is their eating of the forbidden fruit in the garden. But in other instances where the command/fulfillment formula comes into play, a character who generally is obedient becomes more complicated to interpret.

In Numbers 20:7–12 we read about Moses drawing water from a rock to appease the grumbling Israelites in the wilderness:

> The LORD spoke to Moses, saying: *Take the staff*, and assemble the congregation, you and your brother Aaron, and *command the rock before their eyes to yield its water*. Thus you shall bring water out of the rock for them; thus you shall provide drink for the congregation and their livestock.
>
> *So Moses took the staff from before the LORD, as he had commanded him*. Moses and Aaron gathered the assembly together before the rock, and

3. This reminds me of what comes later in the Bible in the book of Job, with the role of the *satan* (the accuser). In Job the *satan* sets out to test the true nature of Job's faith (though note that the serpent in Genesis is not the same figure as the *satan* we find later in the Bible).

> he said to them, "Listen, you rebels, shall we bring water for you out of this rock?" *Then Moses lifted up his hand and struck the rock twice with his staff*; water came out abundantly, and the congregation and their livestock drank. But the LORD said to Moses and Aaron, "Because you did not trust in me, to show my holiness before the eyes of the Israelites, therefore you shall not bring this assembly into the land that I have given them." (NRSV)

Here we find an incongruity between the instruction God gave Moses and Moses's actions. Moses takes the staff "as [God] had commanded him."[4] (We often find this note when instructions are faithfully followed, and this note is most frequently attributed to Moses in the Pentateuch.) But the second part of Moses's response contrasts with God's instruction; where God says to speak to the rock, Moses strikes . . . and strikes again! If we zoom out even further to take in the broader context, we will notice that this water-from-rock miracle is not the first time Moses has brought water from a rock. Earlier in the wilderness wandering, Moses cried out to God for help, and God responded by commanding him similarly to take the staff and *strike* the rock so that there would be water to drink (Exod. 17:4–7). In this earlier instance, we are simply told that "Moses did so" (Exod. 17:6 NRSV). Notably, what Moses got right the first time, he got wrong the second by repeating God's earlier instruction, rather than following those given at this later time.[5]

Maybe this parallel illuminates the true act of disobedience that keeps Moses (and Aaron) from leading ancient Israel into the land of promise? Maybe God's determination that Moses will not enter into the promised land is less about one-off mistaken instructions and more about a deeper

4. Jacob Milgrom observes that the additional comment of "as he had commanded him" in v. 9 "would have been expected before or after the account but not in the middle. Its 'misplacement' is deliberate; up to this point Moses executes God's command; thereafter he deviates from it." Milgrom, *JPS Torah Commentary: Numbers*, 165.

5. It is worth pausing to note the difference between a narrative approach to this story and a text-critical approach, as exemplified in Martin Noth's commentary on the same passage. Though Noth sees the similarities between the Exodus and Numbers accounts of "a water-miracle," he surmises that what we find in Numbers is a priestly redaction (P source) of an older (J source) account because of the many similarities, aside from presence of more priestly material—namely, the appearance of Aaron (Noth, *Numbers*, 144). In the narratival approach, we come to know Moses better as a character in the story; in the text-critical approach, we come to know the editor behind the text. That is not to say there is no place for a critical eye for editors, redactions, and textual development, but the danger of losing the forest for the trees—in our case, losing the Bible as literary artistry—lurks nearby.

commentary on Moses's character as a leader, particularly in this moment? What I find most valuable about attending to the command/fulfillment formula is the way it draws readers beyond straightforward assessment of obedience or disobedience and toward a sense of coming to know characters with more familiarity and relatability. I find it so relatable that part of the issue with Moses's disobedience in Numbers 20 may be attributed to Moses not listening as well as he should have because he thought he knew how this should unfold. How often have I done a similar thing?

In the presence of a command/fulfillment formula, we find an example of the ways that indirect characterizations work in biblical narrative. We are offered clues, and like a detective gathering those clues, we must deduce just what kind of person a character is as a story unfolds. Far from being passive observers, we are invited to get to know these commonplace but not necessarily well-known figures of the Bible.

Types of Characters

We find two general types of characters in stories: round and flat. Round characters offer us multiple dimensions of who they are. Flat characters are one-dimensional, lacking nuance or depth. Flat characters can serve a supporting role in a story, but they usually cannot stand up to the focused attention of a leading role.

A prime example of a flat character is the pharaoh of the exodus story. We are not provided much information about him, except that he is the antagonist of the liberation narrative in the early pages of Exodus. We know him best (and really solely) for his repeated resistance to Moses's plea for the freedom of his people from enslavement. In fact, we are offered pretty much all we need to know about him from Pharaoh's first address to Moses in Exodus 5:2: "Who is the LORD that I should heed him and let Israel go? I do not know the LORD, and I will not let Israel go!" (NRSV).

Here, we learn nearly all we need to know about Pharaoh for the rest of the exodus story. Pharaoh does not know the God of Israel and will not obey this God by releasing the Israelites from enslavement. We are told both of these key points twice in this passage, and they continue to be repeated in dialogue and action in the subsequent chapters. Pharaoh serves as an especially helpful example of a flat character because while we read a lot about him and hear from him in the exodus story, his lack of knowledge (that is, fear) of the God of Israel and his refusal to free God's people remains a constant until the very final plague. The troubling language of God "hardening" Pharaoh's heart adds to the one-dimensional aspect of the leader's characterization.[6] Pharaoh may be given a lot of narrative space, but he isn't given much in the way of a personality. Within the biblical story, he's almost more of a symbol than a person.

Conversely, Hagar serves as an example of a round character, though she has often been treated as a flat character (typecast as a servant woman, mistress, handmaid, etc.) through the history of interpretation. We are introduced to Hagar in Genesis 16 when we are told that she is an Egyptian young woman enslaved by Sarai. Sarai instructs Abram to "go in to" Hagar to impregnate her (Gen. 16:2).[7] As we would understand it today, Abram rapes Hagar. What else would you call a slave-owning man "going in to" an enslaved woman?[8] Once Hagar realizes she is pregnant, the narrator tells us that "she looked with contempt on her mistress" (16:4 NRSV). Sarai responds to this contempt by dealing "harshly" with Hagar—we can presume this harsh treatment involved some kind of verbal, physical, and/or emotional abuse—and Hagar runs away (16:6).[9] The narrative that

6. To delve deeper into what we are to do interpretively and theologically with this language of God hardening Pharaoh's heart, I highly recommend as a starting point Claire Mathews McGinnis's "Hardening of Pharaoh's Heart."

7. Lexically, there is a lot of confusion around how we are to understand the role of Hagar, as she is given three different descriptors in the Genesis narratives, two of which designate some type of slave/handmaiden and a third that designates her as a woman/second wife. Most helpful for our examination here is the shift in designation in Gen. 16. In this chapter, Hagar is first referred to in relation to Sarai, as her handmaiden or slave-girl. Then she is referred to as a woman or second wife of Abraham. While we cannot be sure of the meaning of this change, a best guess is that the change in title reflects a change in innocence for Hagar. In her role as handmaid she is "a girl who is not free, but is as yet untouched, whose duty was primarily to serve the woman of the house," whereas the shift to woman/wife in Gen. 16:3 designates her as "a woman who is not free, and who could be a man's secondary wife" (Koehler, Baumgartner, and Stamm, *Hebrew and Aramaic Lexicon*, 1621). So the change in designation for Hagar from the first verse of Gen. 16 to the third is one from the innocence of girlhood to sexualized womanhood.

8. I realize the weight of this charge, as well as the concern for imposing modern-day valuations on ancient texts. But the narrative itself does not seem to vindicate either Sarai's instruction or Abram's action.

9. Robert Alter notes that the dialogue between Abram and Sarai, after we are told of Hagar's contempt for Sarai, has overtly sexual and direct language. According to Alter, what is most frequently translated as "embrace" in Gen. 16:5 most literally means "'your lap,' often a euphemism for the genital area. The emphasis is pointedly sexual." Alter, *Hebrew Bible*, 1:51n5.

This story of Hagar's pregnancy and then flight to the wilderness does not seem to directly paint Abram and Sarai in the best light, and it indirectly leaves a lot of room for the reader to infer serious moral failings on their part. In fact, the way that Hagar looks at Sarai in Gen. 16:4

follows unfolds an encounter between a messenger from God and Hagar as she is in the wilderness. The messenger tells her to return to Sarai but also that Hagar herself will be the mother of a great multitude (paralleling God's promise to Abram in Gen. 15). Hagar responds with awe and boldness, both giving God a personal name and asking herself in astonishment if this miraculous encounter truly happened (16:13). Hagar then returns to Abram and Sarai. Later, after the birth of Isaac, Hagar finds herself again in the wilderness (21:14). This time she is banished, rather than running away, and she once again meets God as her water skins lie empty on the ground. God comforts her and provides water for her and her son to drink (21:17–19).

Hagar is often an overlooked figure in the cast of characters we find in the Pentateuch (at least within the white Western church context), but at least some of that lack of attention is attributed not to a flat rendering but to a flat reading of her. We come to know a lot about Hagar, both in her actions and in those committed against her. She is raped. After that first injustice, she becomes pregnant, a perpetual reminder of the ways she has been wronged. She is treated poorly for being justifiably upset, so much so that she flees in desperation out into the wilderness. She demonstrates resiliency, boldness, and a deep love for her child. She *is* a heroic figure.

In Delores S. Williams's significant work *Sisters in the Wilderness: The Challenge of Womanist God-Talk*, Williams observes that Hagar has been given great attention by Black American women:

> As I encountered Hagar again and again in African-American sources, I reread her story in the Hebrew testament and Paul's reference to her in the Christian testament. I slowly realized there were striking similarities between Hagar's story and the story of African-American women. Hagar's heritage was African as was black women's. Hagar was a slave. Black American women had emerged from a slave heritage and still lived in light of it. . . . Hagar resisted the brutalities of slavery by running away. Black American women have a long resistance history that includes running away from slavery in the antebellum era. Like Hagar and her child Ishmael,

suggests such a view. Though the phrase is often translated as "[Hagar] looked with contempt on her mistress" (NRSV), the Hebrew text quite literally says that "her mistress appeared small/insignificant in her eyes." This literal translation is more evocative than simply saying that Hagar looked at Sarai with contempt. This translation suggests that Sarai's moral failing was reflected in Hagar's eyes.

> African-American female slaves and their children, after slavery, were expelled from the homes of many slave holders and given no resources for survival. Hagar, like many women throughout African-American women's history, was a single parent. But she had serious personal and salvific encounters with God—encounters which aided Hagar in the survival struggle of herself and her son. Over and over again, black women in the churches have testified about their serious personal and salvific encounters with God, encounters that helped them and their families survive.[10]

Far from being a flat character, Hagar is identified in Williams's work with Black women's struggle and resiliency. In these narratives featuring Hagar, the figures of Abram and Sarai take on the more flattened role, which helps us see Hagar's situation more clearly. We learn the most in these narratives about Hagar's character. It is unsurprising, I think, that those who most identify with Hagar's experience in their own lives can most easily recognize the rich characterization we find in these Genesis stories.

Williams recognizes Black American women's experience in Hagar's trials and perseverance and also offers a broader recognition that as we bring ourselves to the text, we also bring our experiences, which can illuminate or cast shadows on our reading. As I mentioned in the introduction, I came to understand more viscerally the wilderness wanderings of the Pentateuch after moving to central Texas, where dust and lack of water became defining features of life for a big chunk of the year. We bring ourselves to the text; it cannot be helped. But while it can't be avoided, our readings can be enriched by reading alongside others—especially those whose experiences differ from our own. This includes ethnic and racial differences, as well as geographic, cultural, and temporal differences. The invitation to read is a communal invitation, which is why some of my most fruitful studies of Scripture have been around a table with other people. This setting allows us to share different perspectives for a more enriching overall reading of a text.[11]

Adele Berlin expands our exploration of character types by proposing three categories for characters that further delineate flat characters and round ones. She distinguishes between two types of flat characters in

10. D. Williams, *Sisters in the Wilderness*, 2–3.

11. A special note of gratitude to St. James Episcopal Church in Bozeman, Holy Spirit Episcopal Church in Waco, and St. Alban's Episcopal Church in Waco, which have offered me the gift of teaching and learning in community.

addition to round characters, which she identifies as "*full-fledged*." The two subcategories of flat characters are flat as "*type*" and flat as "*agent*."[12] Importantly, these three types of characters (full, type, and agent) should be understood as being on a spectrum rather than as being rigid categories.[13] Berlin points out that a character's type in one story can change in the next.[14] So a rather complex depiction of Moses in the story of the burning bush does not preclude another depiction of Moses simply as a prophetic mouthpiece for God. Or, as we just saw, the central figures of Abram and Sarai can take a back seat in the stories of Hagar.

Berlin understands that for full-fledged characters to be believable as real people "their emotions and motivations are either made explicit or left to be discerned by the reader from hints provided in the narrative. We feel that we know them, understand them, and can, to a large extent, identify with them."[15] Sometimes the full-fledged character looms over us in the text because they occupy a lot of narrative space, but other times these characters make small but punchy appearances, giving us just enough information to create a picture of who they are.

Type characters function as stereotypical roles in a narrative (e.g., the sinful outsider, the power-hungry king, the subservient wife). Exodus's Pharaoh exemplifies this typecasting as an outsider idolatrous ruler who does not recognize the God of Israel. Berlin observes that often type characters represent whole classes of people.[16] The older testament typecasts entire groups such as the Egyptians, the firstborn, or the unclean. We see similar typecasting in the Gospel accounts, particularly in descriptions of the scribes, Pharisees, or leaders. While there are times when a member from this group, like Nicodemus or Joseph of Arimathea, acts as a more rounded character, most frequently the type character functions as a representative of an entire group of people.

Agents are "not important for themselves" but instead "appear in the narrative as functions of the plot or a part of the setting."[17] We know nothing about the agent except how they function to further a story. One of the more memorable examples of an agent is Balaam's donkey in Numbers

12. Berlin, *Poetics and Interpretation*, 23 (italics original).
13. Berlin, *Poetics and Interpretation*, 32.
14. Berlin, *Poetics and Interpretation*, 24.
15. Berlin, *Poetics and Interpretation*, 32.
16. Berlin, *Poetics and Interpretation*, 33.
17. Berlin, *Poetics and Interpretation*, 32.

22:22–35. The donkey functions as, well, a donkey—except this creature *speaks* to Balaam. The donkey addresses his master, saying, "What have I done to you, that you have struck me these three times?" (Num. 22:28) and "Am I not your donkey? Which you have ridden all your life to this day? Have I been in the habit of treating you this way?" (22:30). Within the narrative, the donkey functions as an unusual but useful dialogue partner for Balaam to receive the word he needs to hear. The role of a messenger of God, here fulfilled by a critter, is most frequently fulfilled by an agent called an "angel." We know nothing about these agents except that they serve as a mouthpiece for God. Similarly, we know nothing about the donkey except that this donkey can also, it seems, speak.

A "Haunting Portrait Gallery" of Characters

In his *Poetics of Biblical Narrative*, Meir Sternberg proposes that "the secret of the spell exercised by the Bible over numberless readers through the ages largely resides in its haunting portrait gallery."[18] The central characters we find in the Bible are not flat and wooden characters that predictably act in obedience or disobedience at all times: Abraham lies even as his faith is credited to him as righteousness; Jacob deceives and manipulates his way into a very real blessing intended for another; Moses gets sloppy (maybe even arrogant) despite his long career of obedience. These figures stay with us, haunt us, because they are multidimensional and, at times, unpredictable.

As we come to know these central figures of the Pentateuch, we find they are not perfectly righteous or perfectly evil figures who consistently act in the straightforward and predictable ways we might expect from characters in a religious text. Instead, we discover people as complex as we are, rather unpredictable and complicated in their motivations and actions. We come across characters who reflect ourselves back to us in stories of people chosen by God, people who sometimes demonstrate admirable faithfulness and other times fail spectacularly. Robert Alter shares this sentiment in his case for a literary reading of the Bible. He notes that "what we need to understand better is that the religious vision of the Bible is given depth and subtlety precisely by being conveyed through the most

18. Sternberg, *Poetics of Biblical Narrative*, 254.

sophisticated resources of prose fiction." Alter explains that the figures we find in the Bible "are not simple eponymous counters in an etiological tale (this is the flattening effect of some historical scholarship) but are individual characters surrounded by multiple ironies, artfully etched in their imperfection as well as in their strength."[19] That is, we find altogether *human* figures in biblical figures.

Sternberg offers five key features to look for in gathering up these portraits of characters:

1. Physical characteristics (e.g., Sarah is described as beautiful in Gen. 12:11; Gen. 29:17 notes that Leah has weak eyes and that Rachel is beautiful)
2. Position in society/community (e.g., Joseph is called an adviser in Gen. 41:39–40; Exod. 2:5–10 describes Moses as being raised in the house of Pharaoh)
3. Unique feature or skill set (e.g., Gen. 9:20 notes that Noah is skilled in wine making; Gen. 10:8 describes Nimrod as a mighty warrior; Gen. 25:27 calls Esau a good hunter)
4. Theological comment (e.g., faith is credited to Abraham as righteousness in Gen. 15:6; Gen. 39:3 describes the Lord as being with Joseph)
5. Psychological comment (e.g., Laban accuses Jacob of deception and foolishness in Gen. 31:26–28; Pharaoh identifies Joseph as wise in Gen. 41:39; ancient Israel is described as foolish in Num. 12:11 and Deut. 32:6)[20]

These features help us create a clear outline of a character, which indirect characterization then fills in. Sternberg summarizes these five direct modes of characterization by noting that "they yield a partial picture of the figure and we must round it out by our own efforts, usually at the most essential (intriguing, problematic) spots."[21] I like to think of this process like a coloring page. We are given the general outline of a figure, but it is up to us as readers to fill in that picture with all the details and color we can infer from our repeated readings of these dynamic stories.

19. Alter, *Art of Biblical Narrative*, 23. Here he speaks specifically of the Judah and Jacob-Israel stories in Genesis to draw out the far-from-flat figures we find in the biblical text.

20. Sternberg, *Poetics of Biblical Narrative*, 326.

21. Sternberg, *Poetics of Biblical Narrative*, 327.

As we have seen, biblical narrative offers us mostly indirect means of taking the measure of biblical figures. These indirect means, combined with the sparely told stories, require that we as readers pay attention to the clues and curious inclusions within a story. Sometimes we are helped by the command/fulfillment formula, which offers us insight into the inner workings and motivations that result in a character's outward obedience or disobedience. Other times, we need to attend to characters to whom we may be less inclined to pay attention; in these instances, reading with a broader range of interpreters, like the womanist readings of Hagar, offers us new insights into well-known and possibly overlooked characters. Importantly, the key thing to remember when reading the stories of the Pentateuch is that these figures are not all that different from us. We find characters who struggle with temptation, act with great courage one moment and great cowardice the next, and refuse predictable tropes that sharply delineate the hero from the foe. We come to know the biblical characters in much the same way we come to know one another, by paying attention and understanding the rather complicated and morally muddled nature of taking the measure of someone.

Case Study: The Paradoxical God of Exodus

In the second half of this chapter, I turn to one of the most elusive but also curiously round figures we find in the Pentateuch: the God who identifies himself with Abraham, Isaac, Jacob, and their descendants. The God of the Pentateuch is not like the gods we commonly find in the ancient Near East or in the Greco-Roman pantheon. Many of those gods are known through their rather extravagant and persnickety personalities or they are type characters used to explain why, say, the ground is separated from the sky or the sea. In the Pentateuch, we find a God who stands most often outside, offstage if you will, of the drama of the biblical stories but who is also very much involved in the narrative, most often through a messenger but sometimes by obliquely but resolutely making an appearance on the main stage.

Before we get into some examples of the characterization of God in the Pentateuch, particularly in the book of Exodus, I want to address a concern that may be sending off alarm bells in your head as you read about God as a *character*. During my master's program, I took a seminar on literary approaches to the Old Testament, taught by V. Philips Long.[22] This class was my first real exposure to a literary reading of the Old Testament. By this time in my academic journey, I had grown tired and a bit suspicious of purely historical readings of the Old Testament that seemed to ignore that Scripture was and is a living document for communities of faith and that instead treated it as a historical document like any other historical document. But the idea of artistry—that Scripture was not only a theological witness and guide to faith communities but a work of literary art—was relatively new to me. By this time, I had learned biblical Hebrew well enough to recognize some of the literary play in the text, so that helped as I learned to identify the artistry of ancient Hebrew storytelling. This seminar introduced me to the language of biblical poetics and in many ways did for me what I hope this book does for some of you—that is, opened up a whole new way of reading the Bible. My biggest stumbling block, though, in this course was our conversations around the characterization of God. I found myself very uncomfortable with speaking of God, creator of all things visible and invisible, as simply another character in a story. If some of you are feeling a similar discomfort, I want to affirm that this concern is legitimate. In the same ways that we can historicize Scripture to the point of flattening its dynamism to that of simply an ancient artifact, we can attend to biblical stories as literature to the point of treating this story as just another story among many. We can risk losing the distinctive character of Scripture as *revelation*, of the in-breaking of the transcendent into everyday life. In my investigation here of the God of the exodus, I hope you will see how the characterization of God, when attended to closely, encourages the careful reader to do the opposite of making God just another human character. Instead, we find enigmatic, elusive, even paradoxical descriptions that paint us a picture of a personal God who is still very much God.

In the early chapters of Exodus, we read of the change in circumstances for ancient Israel in Egypt. Genesis had ended with ancient Israel prospering in the land because of Joseph's renown. But those fortunes reversed when "a new king arose over Egypt, who did not know Joseph" (Exod. 1:8 NRSV). Seeing the political threat these non-Egyptians held with their number and influence, the new king subjugates the ancient

22. I highly recommend his book *The Art of Biblical History*, which explores both the literary nature and the historical nature of the Old Testament's historical books.

Israelites, enslaving them and putting them to work in demanding manual labor. Out of this subjugation, Moses is born, and he survives Pharaoh's mandate to kill every newborn Israelite boy. And, of course, many of us know this story well. Moses is raised as an Egyptian but sees the suffering of his people in the land. He ultimately murders an Egyptian who is mistreating an enslaved Israelite. Moses flees into the wilderness, settling in Midian, where he meets his wife, Zipporah.

At the close of this narrative that introduces Moses and sets the scene for the events to come, the focus shifts from Moses to God: "After a long time the king of Egypt died. The Israelites groaned under their slavery, and cried out. Out of the slavery their cry for help rose up to God" (Exod. 2:23 NRSV). Here, we as readers are redirected from Moses as the central figure to God, who hears the suffering of his people. Next we will focus on three passages in Exodus that reveal a round, yet inscrutable characterization of God: the burning bush (3:1–6), Zipporah's appeasement of God's wrath (4:24–26), and God's presence in the dark cloud of Mount Sinai (chaps. 19, 24).

The Burning Bush (Exod. 3:1–6)

> Moses was keeping the flock of his father-in-law Jethro, the priest of Midian; he led his flock beyond the wilderness, and came to Horeb, the mountain of God. There the angel of the LORD appeared to him in a flame of fire out of a bush; he looked, and the bush was blazing, yet it was not consumed. Then Moses said, "I must turn aside and look at this great sight, and see why the bush is not burned up." When the LORD saw that he had turned aside to see, God called to him out of the bush, "Moses, Moses!" And he said, "Here I am." Then he said, "Come no closer! Remove the sandals from your feet, for the place on which you are standing is holy ground." He said further, "I am the God of your father, the God of Abraham, the God of Isaac, and the God of Jacob." And Moses hid his face, for he was afraid to look at God. (Exod. 3:1–6 NRSV)

Even the less well-versed Bible reader likely knows the story of the call of Moses via the burning bush. In response to God hearing the anguished cries of the enslaved Israelites in Exodus 2, God encounters Moses as he leads Jethro's flock up Mount Horeb. A spectacular call narrative ensues. God addresses Moses from a burning bush, a scene literally translated in verse 2 as "a flame of fire in the midst of the bush." Moses looks at this bush and is stunned because the bush is burning but it is not consumed. He looks at the bush and wonders why it is not burnt (v. 3). And then God *speaks* from the burning bush that is not burning, calling to Moses. Once Moses affirms that he is present and listening, God directs Moses to treat this space for what it is: a holy place. Following the startling and miraculous not-burning burning bush, God goes on to tell Moses who he is in concrete and personal terms: "I am the God of your father, the God of Abraham, the God of Isaac, and the God of Jacob" (v. 6). With this pronouncement, we are told that Moses hides his face because he is afraid.

This story is spectacular. We could just as easily examine the characterization of Moses here as that of God. But for our purposes we will attend to how the narrator gives us an indirect but effective portrait of the God who appears to Moses in the burning bush. The most interesting stroke of characterization may be the description of the bush and Moses's inquisitive response. Let us compare a handful of translations to see what is going on here in Exodus 3:2–3:

> Then the angel of the Lord appeared to him in a flame of fire within a bush. As Moses looked, he saw *that the bush was on fire but was not consumed.* So Moses thought, "I must go over and look at this remarkable sight. *Why isn't the bush burning up?*" (CSB)

> And the angel of the Lord appeared unto him in a flame of fire out of the midst of a bush: and he looked, and, behold, the bush burned with fire, and the bush was not consumed. And Moses said, I will now turn aside, and see this great sight, *why the bush is not burnt.* (KJV)

> There the angel of the Lord appeared to him in flames of fire from within a bush. Moses saw that though the bush was on fire it did not burn up. So Moses thought, "I will go over and see this strange sight—*why the bush does not burn up.*" (NIV)

> There the angel of the Lord appeared to him in a flame of fire out of a bush; he looked, and *the bush was blazing, yet it was not consumed.* Then Moses said, "I must turn aside and look at this great sight, and see why *the bush is not burned up.*" (NRSV)

This demonstrates a curious matter of translation: all these versions indicate but do not fully capture the paradoxical nature of Moses's dual response. He sees that the bush was alight but not consumed by fire, and then he asks why the bush is not burned. The phrase "burned up" suggests consumption, which relates to Moses's shock in verse 2 that the bush is *burning* but not *consumed*. Moses responds by wondering why the bush is not *burned*, but translators frequently add the word "up" (i.e., burned up) or translate the word as past tense (i.e., burnt). They do so to correlate Moses's closer examination with consumption by fire. In Hebrew, though, "to burn" and "to consume" are two different verbs. The first verb ("to burn") is specific to what fire does when something is set aflame. "To consume," however, has the broader and more forceful meaning of being eaten up, being devoured, or being no more. In this passage we are told that when Moses takes a closer look, the fire appears to be doing one thing (burning) but not another thing (consuming). The curious matter here is that when Moses speaks aloud what he sees, he does not ask why the fire is not *consuming* the bush but instead why it is not *burning*: "Moses said, 'I must turn aside to see this great sight, why the bush is not burnt'" (3:3).

I do not wish to go too far down a rabbit hole of verb choices, but I do wonder if some indirect characterization is afoot here in Moses's encounter with God in the bush. That is, Moses does not possess the language to fully account for what he encounters. The bush burns but does not burn. Here, we find a character on the main stage who confounds accurate description. Even when he is in the presence of God, standing on holy ground, Moses struggles to capture all that is happening. This incident prefigures the beautiful account in Isaiah 43:2, which assures those in exile that "when you walk through fire you will not be scorched and the flame will not burn you." When God is with you, the impossible burning-yet-not-burning becomes possible and believable. It fits what we know of God through how God is characterized in Scripture.

Interestingly, though, this theophany does not end with the burning bush that is not being consumed, not burning. Instead, what really seems to overcome Moses is God speaking out of the absurdly not-burning burning bush. God speaking demonstrates that he is a concrete figure, the God of Moses's family, of his ancestors, of a particular people that God has chosen for God's own. This concrete expression of the one who speaks from the burning bush pushes Moses beyond curiosity and into the realm of fear. He loses his boldness in the face of the miraculous and instead hides his face. The glory of God, it seems, overwhelms Moses not in stunning miracles but in intimacy. Here we find a characterization of God that is at once paradoxical and particular, confounding and yet intimate. It is rather unsurprising, then, that the story picks up after this theophany with God offering Moses a personal name; God is no longer a God of Moses's ancestors but the God of Moses himself.

In the account of the burning bush, we can see how God is treated as a character in a story—but God is not treated as just any character. We find paradoxical description that points to God's presence in the scene. Despite God being onstage, we still find an indirect characterization that pushes beyond what we know. I am reminded of the way Rowan Williams speaks of representing rather than describing what we encounter. Doing so produces "a way of speaking that may variously be said to seek to embody, translate, make present or re-form what is perceived."[23] In the burning bush encounter, we are given a narrative account of God on the center stage. This account affirms that God is present to Moses in this moment even while remaining distinctively God, one not rendered like anyone else. We are offered this unique story in place of simply not rendering God narratively at all. God is embodied as a character, translated into the story, made present to Moses (and to us) without endangering the distinction between God, creator of all things, and the creatures and creations God has made. God is characterized not only indirectly but paradoxically, in a way that makes God present in the story while also remaining credible as God, the King of the universe.

Zipporah Appeases God's Wrath (Exod. 4:24–26)

> On the way, at a place where they spent the night, the Lord met him and tried to kill him. But Zipporah took a flint and cut off her son's foreskin, and touched Moses' feet with it, and said, "Truly you are a bridegroom of blood to me!" So he let him alone. It was then she said, "A bridegroom of blood by circumcision." (Exod. 4:24–26 NRSV)

Moving from one of the most beautifully enigmatic to one of the most bizarre characterizations of God, here we are introduced to a serious prob-

23. R. Williams, *Edge of Words*, 22.

lem and see it resolved rather cryptically in the space of three verses. One wouldn't be blamed for either quickly skimming over these verses to get to the confrontation between Pharaoh and Moses in Egypt or simply filing this event under strange and inexplicable things God does in the Old Testament. Terence Fretheim helpfully warns us away from skipping over or writing off this story: "The narrator seems to be silent regarding God's motivation [to kill Moses, and possibly his son], though it may be hidden in the difficulties; hence one should be careful not to appeal too quickly to God's mysterious ways."[24] Fretheim uncovers some of these difficulties by insisting that the description of God *attempting* to kill Moses suggests that this action should be understood as a "threat" to Moses and not "a single-minded divine intention for death."[25] That is, Zipporah sees an opening to respond well under the threat, recognizing an opportunity to appease God so that the threat may be removed. The action of circumcising her son and touching the foreskin (which is likely bloody, foreshadowing both the Passover and the atoning power of sacrificial blood in worship) to Moses's "feet" gets to the heart of God's concern. Zipporah here mediates God's desire for his people in the parallel way that Moses will later, when he tells the Israelites to spread blood on their doorposts during the Passover event (12:21–27).[26]

While rather different from the burning bush, this story characterizes God in a similar way. That is, God is presented as elusive yet discernible. God is one whom Zipporah can understand and with whom she can negotiate.

Theophanies on Mount Sinai (Exod. 19, 24)

We have seen the God of the exodus so far characterized as paradoxical, yet approachable; perplexing, yet willing to negotiate. We now turn to the most enigmatic characterization of God in Exodus and arguably in the whole of the Pentateuch: God meeting with Moses on Mount Sinai. Recalling that we are exploring the characterization of God in Exodus, I want us to focus on the ways that we learn about who God is through the stunning yet cryptic descriptions of theophany in Exodus 19 and 24. What we will find is an extension of the paradoxical attributes of God

24. Fretheim, *Exodus*, 78.
25. Fretheim, *Exodus*, 78.
26. Fretheim, *Exodus*, 79.

in the burning bush story, but here the attributes are both more evocative and more splendid.

In Exodus 19, we arrive with ancient Israel at the foot of Mount Sinai after months of wandering the wilderness after liberation from Egypt. We are told without preamble that Moses goes up to God in the mountain (even before God calls to him). This move is unsurprising both because Moses already received one theophany atop a mountain in Exodus 3 and because in the ancient world mountains are often where one goes to meet with a deity. The following chapters document Moses's movement up and down Mount Sinai, communing with God at the top and sharing instructions with the people at the bottom. Notably, God's presence atop the mountain is presented in terms of degree (God is not simply present or absent but displays differing registers of presence), as we will see in both Exodus 19 and 24.

In Exodus 19:9, we find God speaking about how God will come to Moses. Here, we see the degrees of presence. God speaks to Moses but has not yet arrived. It seems that God's speaking and God's presence are characterized as two different but related things. God declares that he will come to Moses in what is translated literally as "a cloud of the cloud." There are actually two different Hebrew words behind these references to clouds. Most often, translators render this phrase as "a dark cloud" or "a thick cloud" because the first mention of "cloud" is often associated with storm clouds or clouds carrying the threat of rain elsewhere in Scripture (e.g., Judg. 5:4; 1 Kings 18:44). However, this is only one use for the term, which can also simply suggest clouds that cast shadows or move swiftly across the sky. The second cloud mentioned in this phrase also designates clouds generally. It is the same word used earlier in Exodus 13 to refer to the pillar of cloud that led ancient Israel through the wilderness by day. Both of these terms for "cloud" are not particularly unusual in the Old Testament, but it is quite unusual for them to appear together. Exodus 19:9 is the only place the two appear together as one construct phrase, despite appearing over thirty and eighty times respectively on their own.

Alter notes this unusual construct, refusing in his own translation to translate the first reference to a cloud as a simple modifier of the second. Instead he translates this pair as "the utmost cloud" because here we find "together two words that mean the same thing and that elsewhere are paired in poetic parallelism. The effect would seem to be a kind of epic intensification."[27] Epic intensification indeed, for here we find God not only communing with Moses but doing so in a way that even the people on the foot of the mountain may hear—God draws very near. In order to narrate the most unique of characters doing the most unusual of things, the storyteller offers us an unusually cloudy cloud.

This strange language does not end how God's presence is rendered in Exodus 19. As the chapter goes on, we are told of a "heavy" or "thick" cloud that comes upon the mountain, along with an epic storm of thunder and lightning that engulfs the mountain with flame and smoke and shakes the entire mountain as God's presence descends on it. This scene of God's presence reinforces Alter's contention that the strange cloud construct in verse 9 is a grand syntactical intensification. Reflecting on this great theophany, Alter recognizes that this "Sinai encounter is imagined as the decisive moment in human history when the celestial and terrestrial realms are brought into panoramic engagement, and as God comes down the mountain, every sort of natural fireworks is let loose, so that trembling seizes not only the people but the mountain itself."[28] To characterize God narratively is to show indirectly, through effects, God as creator and sustainer of the universe. God is characterized here through pushing the natural realm to its limits—fire, smoke, and trembling ensue. To characterize God is to characterize a figure like no other. Here we can see that any concern with making God simply another character in a story is cast off as God is described in the most grand, awe-inspiring, and terrifying of scenes.

Later, in Exodus 24:9, Moses, Aaron and his two sons, and the seventy elders all journey up the mountain. We are told in verse 10 that in going up they *saw* God and lived, something that should not be possible. Yet we are told that they do see, while the narrator also immediately moves their eyes and ours to what lies below God's feet. Here, a spatial shift indirectly captures that God as character is not one to be described except by effects and surroundings: "And they saw the God of Israel. Under his feet there was something *like* a pavement of sapphire stone, *like* the very heaven for clearness" (24:10 NRSV). Even the description of what lies below God's feet is obliquely rendered, with the double phrasing of "something *like*" something else. Alter rightly notes that "for this zone

27. Alter, *Hebrew Bible*, 1:292n9.
28. Alter, *Hebrew Bible*, 1:293n16.

touched by the divine, direct linguistic reference is not possible, and so the writer uses double simile."[29] Whatever it means to see God, it does not mean an ordinary and direct kind of sight.

While it is tempting to linger in these passages longer, I think we have witnessed enough to see how in these Mount Sinai theophanies, God is characterized through unusual phrasing, extreme description, and poetic expression. God is treated as a character in this story, one who speaks, arrives, effects, and even in some obscure way is seen. This characterization of God follows a pattern of characterization in the Hebrew Bible, where a figure is rendered indirectly. But to characterize God is also to push the limits of the usual modes of description. We find here a "character" in God who can be known but not in the usual ways, who can be spoken of but only by pushing the boundaries of ordinary language, who can take center stage but not without turning that stage (in the spirit of Emily Dickinson) slant.

Conclusion

We have seen in this chapter the way that the "less is more" approach invites us as readers into not only the narrative world but character building in the Pentateuch. An awareness of the frequently indirect modes of characterization helps us to see familiar biblical figures in new light and attend to lesser-known ones with curiosity and empathy. Biblical Hebrew narrative offers us characters that are not all that different from us. They have complex motives, are conflicted in loyalties, and function sometimes as transgressors and other times as exemplars of faith. My hope is that a greater appreciation for the ways we come to know characters in the Pentateuch will help draw us more deeply into these stories, so that we may come to know ourselves and ourselves before God more honestly and clearly.

So far, we have focused on features of biblical Hebrew narrative that we find across the stories of the Pentateuch. Brevity, pacing, and characterization play important roles in the artistry of all of these biblical stories, and understanding how they function equips us as readers to dive more deeply into them. There are other features that are less ubiquitous but just as evocative that show up in the biblical text. It is to those features that I now turn.

29. Alter, *Hebrew Bible*, 1:315n10.

CHAPTER 5

Complexity in Characterization

Introduction

By now, it should be clear that the stories in the Pentateuch are not simply caricatures of figures of faith or villainous anti-heroes set on complete destruction. Instead, what we find in these stories is much like what we find in real life: people with diverse and conflicting intentions that make it challenging at times to make clear-cut moral demarcations. This is why Sternberg deems the Old Testament characters to be "a haunting portrait gallery."[1] They are haunting, at least in part, because they possess a familiarity, a recognizability to us as readers. We see ourselves in them. We are familiar with their complex motivations, mischievousness, faithfulness, and the intricacies that inform their decisions to act and speak as they do. The older testament is often underappreciated for its relatable quality; it is too frequently deemed to be an obscure or antiquated text.

The best way I have found to heighten appreciation is to encourage people to read these stories slowly and with the same attention we might give our favorite work of fiction or poetry. To suspend what we think we already know and instead come to these stories with as fresh of eyes as we can muster to see something new. Here is where different translations can prove helpful. Reading a familiar story in a less familiar translation can help us gain new insight. Reading a story out loud at a measured pace or listening to one being read to you can also help you encounter a story

1. Sternberg, *Poetics of Biblical Narrative*, 254.

from a different angle. For example, I often find myself noting something new or curious when a familiar Bible story is read aloud as part of the Sunday lectionary cycle during a church service. The lector's intonation, pacing, or emphasis aids me in hearing an old story anew. Importantly, to read these stories with focused attention involves an intentional choice to read them as literary artistry rather than simple didactic instruction. Of course, there are lessons to be learned from biblical stories, but these lessons are not always obvious and sometimes can require focused attention by the reader.

I once again turn to Tolkien's *The Lord of the Rings* because what he offers us in this masterpiece is its own haunting portrait gallery full of characters that resist unambiguous casting as hero, victim, or villain. Samwise Gamgee's greatest strength in this story is his loyalty to Frodo, but this same gift of friendship to Frodo proves to be a cruelty toward Gollum. Gandalf's wisdom and discernment does not preclude him from fully recognizing the danger that his mentor, Saruman, has switched sides. Boromir's heroic and courageous spirit blinds him to his own weakness, yet he still proves himself to be a hero in his final moments. And on it goes. These well-rounded characters possess multiple dimensions to their personhood, permitting them to be both strong and weak, discerning and dense, loving and cruel—much like each of us.

We find this same complexity in the figures of the Pentateuch. This attention to complexity should not presuppose that the narrator is playing games with us as readers so much as drawing out how in the same ways our motives are sometimes hidden or complex, so too are the motives of the figures that fill the pages of the Pentateuch. In mentioning "complexity," I allude to something akin to Jesus's saying that understanding comes to those with eyes to see and ears to hear (e.g., Mark 8:18). Scripture is not simply an instruction manual or a moralistic allegory. Scripture is an invitation for us to journey with those who (sometimes literally) journey with God, to learn more about both the God we love and the people we are.

More Agents, More Problems

In biblical Hebrew narrative, we most frequently find stories about two figures. We can think of it like a staged drama, where we often find only two "actors" onstage. Of course, God is often just offstage, making illusory appearances through messengers (angels), a kind of voice-over (e.g., the prophetic formula where "the word of the LORD" comes to a prophet). In the Pentateuch, God even appears in the form of inanimate objects, like pillars of cloud and smoke. Onstage, though, we usually have two human actors: Adam and Eve, Abraham and Sarah, Jacob and Esau, and so on. Because biblical narrative is made up of dialogue and is action driven, it makes sense not to have too many conversation partners in any one scene.

While this is not always the case, when characterization is more complicated, more fraught, we frequently find more than two people onstage. In the prior chapter, we explored the curious dynamics among Eve, the serpent, and Adam. In Genesis 3, we find a conversation between Eve and the serpent, as Adam seemingly looks on, only performing narrated action when Eve hands him the fruit, which he eats without a word at the close of Genesis 3:6. A literal translation makes clear just how inactive Adam was throughout the previous temptation narrative through the narrator's note that, oh yes, Adam was also there: "And she gave also to her man *with her* and he ate." The inclusion of the comment "*with her*" casts a shadow back on the earlier verses, painting a picture of Adam shoulder to shoulder with Eve as she spoke with the serpent. Adam's reserved role in this scene would make for a comical comment, if not for the seriousness of the moment, when God asks him how he knows he is naked, and Adam responds, "The woman you *set* with me, she *gave* it to me . . ." (3:12). Adam blames Eve and God for what transpired. The italicized verbs "set" and "gave" are the same verb in Hebrew. Adam creates a verbal chain of blame, from Eve's folly to God's gift of companionship. She gave it to me, Adam says, because you gave her to me.

But, at the same time, we see a kind of misdirection at work. While Adam tells us that he is not to blame, the narrator made clear a few verses earlier that Adam stood around throughout the entire dialogue between Eve and the serpent. The addition of "with her" in Genesis 3:6 implicates Adam as privy to the temptation, and Adam's response to God digs him deeper into this hole of a willful choice not to choose. As Eve's God-gifted partner, he is meant to support her in the way of faithfulness when confronted with cunning false arguments (and Eve has the same obligation to Adam). We may find ourselves giving Adam a kind of side-eye as we read back through Eve's dialogue with the serpent and wonder what exactly Adam was up to this entire time. The narrator encourages us to do this through the discreet but pointed note that Adam was "with her." She did not need to go find Adam in another part of the garden or call out to him because he was too far away to simply be handed the fruit. We find a form of misdirection here that does not let Eve off the hook but also does not let us ignore Adam's role in this act of disobedience.

Of course, throughout the history of interpretation this passage has come to mean all kinds of things, from Eve reflecting all women's weakness and emotionalism in terms of temptation to Adam's failure to be a so-called man in this couple by serving as the decision maker. This story has served and continues to serve as a tool of subjugation and a theological account of gender. I realize it is hard for some of us to read this story without jumping to these interpretations—or without jumping to extreme reactions against them. I want to invite us to try to read with fresh eyes, wondering about this story not as an allegory or prescription for gender construction or married life but instead as a story that is buzzing with interpretive possibilities. We find three characters onstage; two are at the center engaging in active dialogue while another looks on—not entirely forgotten but in the shadows. What opportunities might we find here to see Sternberg's haunting portrait gallery not only in Eve but in the side-eye glance to Adam? What interpretive fruit might be missed if we move too quickly from the drama of this narrative to the grand implications that this story also invites?

Case Study: Genesis 27

Jacob

The story of Jacob's stealing his brother's blessing in Genesis 27 offers us a picture of familial dysfunction that would be right at home in a modern-day melodrama. The family conflict around Isaac's intended blessing involves favoritism, intrigue, and striving between brothers and parents alike. The deception results in a successfully stolen blessing, one of the more troubling outcomes in the biblical narratives because God appears to honor what has been received through dishonesty. The story is also unusual because it involves four characters in one story, all playing important roles in the orchestrated deception. Here we move beyond the side-eye we find in a passing narrative comment to try and discern the intentions and dynamics at play in the shadows of a rather remarkable sham.

Genesis 27 begins with the gray and weak-eyed Isaac, most beloved son of Abraham and Sarah, calling for his beloved elder son, Esau. This scene opens with quite a bit of family baggage in tow: the tension between Isaac's two sons, Esau and Jacob, begins even before they are born with a tussle in Rebekah's womb and God's proclamation that the elder son will serve the younger (Gen. 25), along with the rather odd story of Jacob the younger receiving Esau the elder's birthright for a bowl of stew. All of this family history comes to bear as Jacob misleads his father into giving him a blessing intended for his brother.

The story we read in Genesis 27 is more substantial in details than many of the other stories we find concerning Jacob's life. In this story we're able to take a long look at an intimate domestic scene, with the drama of scheming and deception unfolding before us. Before he dies, Isaac prepares to give Esau a special blessing by asking his son to go out and hunt some game so that there may be a tasty meal for Isaac and a subsequent blessing for Esau. The narrative is rather straightforward until we come to Genesis 27:5, where we are told that Rebekah lurked in the shadows and eavesdropped on this conversation. Upon hearing Isaac's plan, Rebekah immediately formulates her own scheme to trick her husband into blessing her favored son, Jacob, instead of Esau. Rebekah is successful in her ploy. Jacob receives Esau's blessing, and Esau, in stunningly dramatic fashion, just misses the ruse and is consequently devastated when he receives the news that his blessing has been given to his younger brother. Isaac, realizing what has happened, gives Esau what could be best described as a half-blessing, entailing nothing of the magnitude of the Abrahamic blessing he gave to Jacob. Esau, understandably fuming with anger, vows to kill Jacob. Jacob, just as understandably, flees.

Though this story is most well-known for Jacob's deception, it indirectly but clearly implies failure by two other actors: Rebekah and Isaac. While these implications are not conclusive in terms of characterization, they do invite us to give Rebekah and Isaac the side-eye, as it were, much like we gave Adam in the Genesis 3 narrative. Looking askance at them in this drama offers us more interpretive possibilities and invites us to see these parents as more like us: imperfect, complicated, and conflicted at key moments in our lives. In the case of Isaac, we find one of the great patriarchs of the Abrahamic blessing seemingly impotent and undiscerning at a crucial moment. And, from the start of the story, we find Rebekah lurking in the shadows. A close reading evidences that she is there throughout the story and is functioning as the true trickster—arguably helping us to more readily identify where Jacob gets both his intelligence and his cunning.

Isaac

This story of a stolen blessing functions to finalize the shift in the story cycle, as it is sometimes called, from Isaac to Jacob. A story cycle can be understood as a series of stories centering primarily on one protagonist. As examples, consider the earlier stories about Noah's life in Genesis 6:9–9:29 or about Abraham in Genesis 12:1–25:11.[2] In these chapters, we find a series of short stories about the feats, failures, and blessings of key figures in the unfolding biblical story. Looking ahead, we find a similar pattern in stories centered on Joseph (Gen. 37:2–36; Gen. 39:1–Exod. 1:6), Moses (Exod. 2:1–Deut. 34:8),[3] and Joshua (Deut. 34:9–Josh. 24:31). These cycles overlap, which allows for the next key figure to be introduced during the life of the central character in a cycle. Demarcating the story cycles is more of an art than a science, as we must allow for stories—say, about Moses to Joshua—to cross-fade, with Joshua coming to the fore as Moses steps back.

Curiously, Isaac's story cycle remains undeveloped and never fully stands on its own, apart from his father Abraham's and his son Jacob's stories. That is, Isaac never truly serves as the hero of his own cycle. Let's do a quick survey to demonstrate this: Isaac is born in Genesis 21:3, then reappears in the narrative of his binding in Genesis 22. In this story, Isaac plays a very small role. He walks with his father, carries the wood for the burnt offering, asks about the whereabouts of the burnt offering, continues on the journey silently after receiving a cryptic response from his father, then finds himself bound and placed on the wood he once carried as his father takes up the slaughtering knife. Maybe he is simply fulfilling the role of obedient son, but his silence here is rather curious. We will explore this story in more detail in the next chapter, but for now the important thing to note is that even when Isaac is center stage, he is quiet, passive,

2. The Abraham cycle example demonstrates that these cycles can overlap and are fuzzy at times in terms of one ending and another beginning. For these examples, I am using the death of the figure as the formal close of the cycle. In the case of Abraham, the majority of the narratives featuring Abraham ended in the previous chapter.

3. Moses is a unique case as his life is traced across four of the five books of the Pentateuch.

and seemingly incredibly naive, scared, or aloof as he becomes the sacrifice he asked about earlier in the story.

As Isaac later comes of age, Abraham seeks out a wife for Isaac in Genesis 24. Abraham sends out a servant for this task. This narrative follows the pattern of a type-scene, which Robert Alter describes as "the perplexing fact that in biblical narrative more or less the same story often seems to be told two or three or more times about different characters, or sometimes even about the same character in different sets of circumstances."[4] Alter helpfully compares the type-scene to a movie genre like the Western, where certain features appear across different stories. The same kind of genre distinction appears in a biblical type-scene, where it is not unusual for a similarly patterned story to occur with different characters at different times in different locations. We find the future spouse identified at a watering hole, but what is unusual for this kind of type-scene is that Isaac himself is not present at the well. This is the only type-scene of this kind where the servant is present rather than the seeker.[5] Abraham's reluctance to send Isaac on this wife-seeking mission may be attributed to a desire for Abraham and Isaac not to be separated so soon after Sarah's death, but nonetheless Isaac is absent in action and dialogue for the narrative of his courtship with Rebekah.

Notably, Isaac makes no appearance until the last two verses of a lengthy chapter, when in Genesis 24:66–67 we read that the servant reports back to Isaac about Rebekah: "Then Isaac brought her into his mother Sarah's tent. He took Rebekah, and she became his wife; and he loved her" (24:67 NRSV). In Genesis 25, Abraham dies, and here we might expect a clear transition to Isaac as the central figure in the subsequent stories, but instead we find one verse in this chapter where Isaac takes center stage, praying for Rebekah's barren womb. The Lord hears his prayer in Genesis 25:21 before Jacob (and Esau) enter the scene. In Genesis 26, readers are offered three vignettes. These vignettes confirm that Isaac continues the story that began with his father Abraham:

1. God confirms that the promise made to Abraham continues with Isaac (26:1–6).
2. Isaac commits a deception similar to his father's by claiming his wife as his sister for political and economic advantage (26:7–17).

4. Alter, *Art of Biblical Narrative*, 58.
5. Cotter, *Genesis*, 167.

3. Isaac is reaffirmed as continuing the Abrahamic blessing, which is recognized by God and a foreign king, as well as by having a physical place to belong in the land (26:18–33).

In Genesis 27–28, the short-lived Isaac cycle ends with the story of a stolen blessing. Isaac's death is recorded later in Genesis, after Jacob and Esau reunite in 35:27–29: "Jacob came to his father Isaac at Mamre, or Kiriath-arba (that is, Hebron), where Abraham and Isaac had resided as aliens. Now the days of Isaac were one hundred eighty years. And Isaac breathed his last; he died and was gathered to his people, old and full of days; and his sons Esau and Jacob buried him" (NRSV).

What I want us to notice about this brief survey is that we learn very little about Isaac. The sense we get from these stories is more that the narrator wants to reinforce continuity with Abraham and the promise than convey anything distinct about Isaac as a person. You can especially see this emphasis on continuity in the verses regarding his death, as Jacob and Esau bury him in the same place where Abraham and Isaac resided. In terms of characterization, Isaac is best described as a flat character. We know very little about his distinctives. In fact, how we come to know him best is through his inaction: inaction in his childhood binding, inaction in finding his wife, and, most pointedly, inaction in his elderly years to thwart the conniving of his wife and son to steal a blessing.

Beyond inaction, it is also possible to interpret Isaac here as an *active* failure. One scholar, Craig A. Smith, looks to the chiastic structure of Genesis 27 to emphasize Isaac's failing.[6] A chiasm is one way of viewing the structure of a literary work in terms of mirroring, so the central point or interpretive key is understood as lying at the center of the narrative. While chiastic structures can be interpreted in ways that skew a story's meaning or subvert the artistry that lies outside of structural elements, chiasm can prove helpful in viewing a story from another angle because it offers us readers a way to step back and attend to a story's structure as an aid in meaning-making.

Smith identifies a chiasm in Genesis 26:34–28:9 (with Esau's marriages as the narrative bookends) that places Isaac blessing Jacob in 27:26–29 at the center of the overarching narrative. Here is how Smith sees the chiasm:

6. C. Smith, "Reinstating Isaac," 130–34.

- **A.** Esau marries (26:34–35).
  - **B.** Isaac calls (*ka-rah*) for a son (here Esau) and commands him to "go" on a search (for game) (27:1–4).
    - **C.** Rebekah involves herself, devising a plan to aid Jacob (27:5–17).
      - **D.** The deception is enacted (27:18–25).
        - **E.** Isaac blesses Jacob (27:26–29).
      - **D′.** The deception is discovered (27:30–41).
    - **C′.** Rebekah involves herself, devising a plan to save Jacob (27:42–46).
  - **B′.** Isaac calls (*ka-rah*) for a son (here Jacob) and commands him to "go" on a search (here for a wife) (28:1–7).
- **A′.** Esau marries (28:8–9).[7]

Notice the way the chiasm repeats themes leading up to and following the central event of blessing: Esau marries, Isaac calls for a son and sends him off to search something out, Rebekah gets involved by making a plan. These repetitive themes serve as a road map to the key part of the story. Smith argues that Isaac as blesser serves as the interpretive key for the story as a whole: Isaac sits at the center of the chiasm and actively blesses the wrong son. This central action signals to the reader an aged patriarch who has failed to live up to the gold standard of his father.[8] Centering Isaac as blesser places Isaac's failure more broadly as a patriarch in stark relief.

Smith concludes that "only by understanding the author's negative evaluation of Isaac as patriarch in this narrative does it become possible to properly understand the place of other characters in this text."[9] Rebekah, then, is the overstepping wife thrust into an inappropriate handling of the situation because of Isaac's failed role as head of his family. Jacob is the easily manipulated son who looks to his mother rather than his father for reception of a blessing that has been prophesied as his own. Esau's situation, marrying unsuitable women and becoming the black sheep of the family, is rooted in his father's failure to clearly communicate what it means to be in the line of Abraham. Smith's reading may be overconfident in the work this chiasm accomplishes, as he insists that only through it

7. C. Smith, "Reinstating Isaac," 131. Bold added to emphasize the chiastic structure.
8. C. Smith, "Reinstating Isaac," 131–32.
9. C. Smith, "Reinstating Isaac," 132.

can the other characters be *properly* rendered. But his reading does open up the ways misdirection in terms of characterization might work in a story like this one. If we turn our attention to Isaac, we see Jacob in a new light. Not so much as a trickster but more as a competitive son with a failure for a father. Whether Isaac turns out to be a man of inaction, failure, or some combination of the two, the story of stolen blessing offers us a clue as to why Isaac, of "Abraham, Isaac, and Jacob" fame, receives so modest a story cycle.

In Genesis 27, we find that the deception was not executed perfectly. Isaac recognized that the food was acquired and prepared much quicker than he expected (v. 20) and that the voice of the son sounded like Jacob, rather than Esau (v. 22); Isaac even asks, "Are you really my son Esau?" (v. 24). It seems rather unusual for the narrator to include these moments of hesitancy if we are meant to believe that Isaac was truly and fully deceived. Instead, we find in Isaac either a man so distrustful of his family that he is suspicious of being cheated or a man who has sufficient clues that something is awry but is too apathetic to act on his suspicion. In either case, Isaac gifts the greatest gift he could give to the wrong son. This unfolding of Isaac's role in the deception offers a fuller, if less-flattering, picture of Isaac the patriarch than we get elsewhere in Genesis.

Rebekah

Earlier, in Genesis 25, we find a description of Jacob and Esau coming of age that makes clear the link between fraternal tension and parental preference: "When the boys grew up, Esau was a skillful hunter, a man of the field, while Jacob was a quiet man, living in tents. Isaac loved Esau, because he was fond of game; but Rebekah loved Jacob" (Gen. 25:27–28 NRSV). These brothers, dramatically different in temperament, reflect a difference in preference between their parents. With this knowledge of parental preference, along with Rebekah's spying in Genesis 27, we as readers can infer some of the fraught family dynamics lurking in the shadows of this great deception.

Poet Yakov Azriel imagines the unnarrated relationship between Rebekah and her less-favored son, Esau, with these devastating lines:

> After he slithered up to my Sabbath
> candles,

Grinning,
Chuckling,
And blew them out,
I slapped him.
Hard.

"*You hit me*!"
He, as astonished as I—
  The perfect mother
  With the patience to water
    caravans of camels—
Could hit,
Would hit,
My son.

"*You hit me*!"
And he began shaking;
His body, unraveling,
Collapsed;
As if all his stars had vanished
And all his bows were snakes;
As if all his vines had withered
And all his seas were ice.

"*You hit me*!"
I stretched out my hand
To his shoulder.
"*Don't touch me*!"
The boy turned and ran out to the field
Sobbing.
Ashamed.
(Of himself?
Of me?)

I lie down on my bed.
And I know:
After I hit my son,
Sabbath candles
Will never give light,
Never shine
For him,

My son,
Again.[10]

Azriel captures what can only be supposed from the biblical text regarding the tension between a mother and her less-preferred son. Her willingness to take Isaac's blessing for her favored son in Genesis 27 only adds to this imagined scene of familial dysfunction. The imagined space is a hard one to inhabit for many reasons: we all have our own baggage in terms of broken family systems; we may desire to view this family (who is key in the birth of God's chosen people) positively; and, most acutely, we as readers know that God foresaw that Jacob would win out over Esau, and God appears to honor the deception by truly blessing Jacob (something that is confirmed in Gen. 28 when God appears to Jacob in a dream at Bethel). Does God choose to work through deception, even violence, to fulfill covenant promises?

Maybe the level of disdain in Azriel's poem fills in the gaps too much. Even so, it offers us an example of the narrative's invitation to attend to textual clues for understanding the characters in deep, complicated, and altogether human ways. We are given quite a bit of information about this family, which offers us an invitation to wonder why Rebekah does what she does in Genesis 27 and how Esau may have felt at this moment—beyond the readily apparent anger toward his brother. Might he have guessed that his brother's deception was also his mother's doing? What did he think of the father who made such a grievous and careless mistake? What was family life like between Isaac, Rebekah, and Esau after Jacob ran away?

In Genesis 27, we find the family dynamics on display when we are told that Rebekah secretly listened to Isaac's instruction to Esau and then reported this conversation to Jacob. Notice how this account is constructed in Genesis 27:5–6, and in particular take note of the use of possessives (indicated by italics):

5a: and Rebekah was listening to Isaac speak to Esau *his son* . . .
5b: [Esau then sets out to find game.]
6a: and Rebekah said to Jacob *her son*:
6b: "Behold! I heard *your father* speak to *your brother* . . ."

10. Azriel, "Rebecca and Esau," 245. Reprinted with permission of Indiana University Press.

In verse 5, we are given two sons, *his son* and *her son*, reinforcing the favoritism we were told about earlier. The narrator here uses possessives to divide the room between those inside of it and those outside of it.

Rebekah's words to Jacob in the second half of verse 6 suggest a shift of point of view, from the narrator's attribution of Esau as Isaac's and Jacob as Rebekah's. Here Rebekah tells Jacob that these are *your* father and brother. This brilliant rhetorical device places Jacob at the center of the action for deception and blessing. Arguably the greatest takeaway from the narrator's inclusion of possessives is that they create a picture of a broken family system (see fig. 5.1). Isaac, Jacob, and Esau all belong to one another in this narrative. As you continue to read through this story of deception, you see the ways that possessives guide us back and forth between characters, more fully drawing out who is whose and the wrongdoing both rendered and received.

Figure 5.1

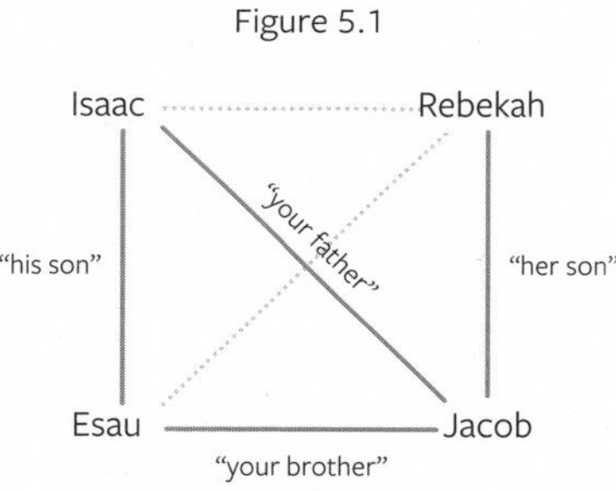

It is worth pausing here to note that the inclusion of *his son*, *her son*, *your father*, and *your brother* were not necessary in this story. Recall that biblical Hebrew narrative is characterized by brevity; it does not go for the "more is more" approach in terms of storytelling. The use of the possessive offers us a clue as to how to read this story (and we don't need to know Hebrew to catch this inclusion!). Rebekah's taking less ownership in the setup for deception is magnified by the fact that in the execution and fallout of the deception we find descriptions of Esau as *her son*: "And she took the finest garments of *her elder son* Esau" (Gen. 27:15); "and the words of *her older son* Esau were told to Rebekah" (27:42). The narrator seems to want to make a point that Rebekah's actions were not only *for* her favored son but *against* the other one.

Hebrew author and poet Menashe Levin invites us deeper into Rebekah and Isaac's relationship with their sons by leaning into the presence of the phrase "my son." First, Isaac speaks to Esau:

> "Esau, my son!" . . . "See how I have aged, my son!" . . . "And I cannot know the day of my death, my son!" . . . "My son, there were days when you climbed out of the narrow places in the mountains." . . . "My son, and at night you take the pieces of roast meat from off the glowing coals." . . . "My son, take your bow . . ."[11]

Esau then joyfully responds, "Ha, my father! Ha, father mine!"[12] Mirroring father and elder son, Rebekah then says to Jacob:

> "Jacob, my son! . . . My son! My son!" . . . "How lovely are your flocks, my son!" . . . "You, my son, are more beautiful than your flock! And now my son, listen to me!" . . . "My son, I shall make delicate food for your father." . . . "And you, my son, shall take the blessing of your father and not Esau, *my son and not my son, your brother and not your brother*." . . . "My son, take two goats from among your goats" . . . "so that he may bless you, my son!"[13]

Notice the conflicted nature of the italicized portion. Rebekah finds herself in a maternal tension with an allegiance to Jacob that might seem commendable, except that it disrupts one of the most natural of sentiments: the love of a parent for a child. For Rebekah, to love one son is to disavow another. For Jacob, to love his mother is to disavow his brother.

Importantly, Levin's reading complicates any notion of Rebekah as a typecast character in this story. She is more complex here than a woman who simply coldheartedly puts one child before another. Instead, we find maternal tension within Rebekah. This tension allows us to attend to her villainous action here without making her a villain, and it permits Rebekah to retain her commendable characterization more broadly in the biblical story, even though she is not acting commendably here. Rebekah, like us, has complicated and conflicting priorities.

11. Levin, "Isaac Blesses Jacob and Esau," 309–10.
12. Levin, "Isaac Blesses Jacob and Esau," 310.
13. Levin, "Isaac Blesses Jacob and Esau," 311–12 (italics added).

Figure 5.2. *Isaac Blessing Jacob; Esau Returning from the Hunt*. From the Haggadah for Passover, fourteenth century.

Visual artistic depictions of this stolen blessing pick up on Rebekah's role in the deception. Sometimes, the artist collapses the scene of Rebekah's eavesdropping and instructions to Jacob with the deceptive act itself. A fourteenth-century illuminated manuscript (where images of a biblical scene surround and expound on the biblical text) offers us a fine example of picturing Rebekah as the master schemer of this narrative (see fig. 5.2).

Notice how the four figures in this image occupy three spaces: inside the home, outside the home, and further beyond with the demarcation of a tree. Jacob resides at the home's threshold with Rebekah standing behind him but also reaching out with her hand on Jacob's arm, an arm also touched by Isaac. Well outside the central action, we find Esau already showing puzzlement at what he will find when he returns home. The artist captures the whole of the narrative sequence with one image: Rebekah eavesdropping, Isaac blessing, Jacob deceiving, and Esau snubbed.

A similarly evocative image comes from Gustave Doré's Bible (1866), where Rebekah's face is hidden from view as she makes sure Esau does not appear on the scene amid the blessing (see fig. 5.3 on the next page). The only face we can see in this image is Isaac's, a rather ironic note as Isaac's blindness is what allows this duplicity to occur. In this depiction, Rebekah is placed in the room where the stolen blessing occurs. Doré's

Figure 5.3. *Isaac Blesses Jacob (Gen. 27:1–27)*. From Doré's English Bible, 1866.

rendering not only brings Rebekah into the room but makes Jacob less notable, keeping his face turned away and occupying less noticeable space in the image than Rebekah or Isaac. Adding dimension to Jacob's role, Doré shrouds Rebekah in darkness, Isaac in light, and Jacob in a mixture of the two. Jacob is covered both in the darkness of deception and in the light of blessing. Esau, on the other hand, is nowhere to be found. In tandem with our earlier reading of Isaac, it is clear that this family system is not a healthy one, and while we often recall this story as one about Jacob's stealing of a blessing, there is much more to attend to.

In the end, maybe only Esau comes out of this story in a favorable light, free of any wrongdoing. My hope is that attention to Rebekah and Isaac helps us see the complexity of characterization, particularly when there are a number of agents acting at the same time. We find an invitation here to wonder about characters without needing to give any of these characters a rubber stamp of blame or absolution.

Conclusion

In this chapter, I focused on the sometimes complicated nature of characterization in the Pentateuch and the invitation in that complication for us as readers to wonder and wander around in the text. I have used poetry and artwork in this chapter to demonstrate how different angles of a story and its characters can be drawn out and experienced from a different viewpoint—in a similar way to reading different translations of the same text or hearing a text read aloud. Different perspectives attending to a shared text help us to experience a familiar story anew.

The story of stolen blessing in Genesis 27 demonstrates the very human character of biblical narrative. Attention to characterization not only enriches stories but offers us as readers a way to connect the stories in the Bible with our own lives. It provides a way to see ourselves reflected back to us in broken families and conflicting commitments. The complexity of characterization in biblical narrative might reassure us that the world has not changed all that much since ancient times and that the grace of God that is working even in rather imperfect systems in these narratives might also be at work in our own lives. In tandem with my larger argument, we see that complex characterization offers us interpretive riches if we give the artistry of these stories attention and time to do its work.

CHAPTER 6

The Grotesque

Introduction

In 1956, Flannery O'Connor wrote a letter to Eileen Hall, the book editor for her diocesan newspaper. While we have only O'Connor's letter to Hall available to us, we can surmise from O'Connor's response that the book editor was concerned about the shocking subject matter in O'Connor's stories, especially for younger readers. O'Connor begins her reply to Hall by stating that she once shared this concern that her stories were altogether too much: "When I first began to write I was much worried about this thing of scandalizing people, as I fancied that what I wrote was highly inflammatory."[1] She continues with what was likely an unexpected retort. Rather than defending her stories' scandalous nature by appealing to her own role as an artist, she points to Scripture: "If a novelist wrote a book about Abraham passing his wife Sarah off as his sister—which he did—and allowing her to be taken over by those who wanted her for their lustful purposes—which he did to save his skin—how many Catholics would not be scandalized by the behavior of Abraham? The fact is that in order to not be scandalized, one has to have a whole view of things, which not many of us have."[2] What she means by the "whole view of things" is the

1. O'Connor, *Habit of Being*, 142.
2. O'Connor, *Habit of Being*, 143.

reality of the world before God, what she calls "the mystery of existence."[3] Part of that mystery is the reality of sin, she argues, for we cannot reflect on the crucifixion—arguably the crux of the Christian claim of what is true—and not attend to sin or, for that matter, gore. O'Connor contends that if we are not in some way scandalized, we entirely miss the point of the Christian faith.

I have always loved that O'Connor points to the story of Abraham and Sarah as an example of a scandalous story. Attending to the stories themselves, as O'Connor does, means that sometimes we are confronted with descriptions of events that are shocking, disgraceful, and even monstrous. These scandalous moments place in stark relief the inherent goodness of the world and the reality of a diminishment or twisting of that goodness. Near the close of her letter, O'Connor writes that what she finds indefensible in storytelling is when "right is held up as wrong, or wrong as right."[4] It is confusion of right and wrong—not scandal, violence, or gore—that is her real concern regarding stories that depict the possibility of God at work in the world.

I begin this chapter with Flannery O'Connor because she has much to teach us about the use of the disturbing and grotesque as ways of speaking truly and artistically about how God might work in the world. She recognizes that many who find offense in stories like hers may also be offended by their own Scriptures, if they look closely enough. Again, Scripture is a "haunting portrait gallery" of humanity and is not made up of blameless figures who never know temptation, manipulation, or violence. It is also an account of a God, creator of the world, perfecter of all things, in relationship with this haunting portrait gallery of characters.

O'Connor also offers us more than a call to attend to the scandal embedded in Scripture. She helps us see how God's work in the world, the presence or possibility of grace, often shows itself in storytelling through the unusual, strange, and grotesque. That is, that which is most pure, perfect, and complete shows its nature in stark relief to the chaotic and disordered nature of our world. In an essay about the use of the grotesque in Southern fiction, O'Connor notes that a writer interested in the mysterious workings of God in the created world will lean into what lies just beyond concrete description:

3. O'Connor, *Habit of Being*, 143.
4. O'Connor, *Habit of Being*, 144.

> The meaning of a story does not begin except at a depth where adequate motivation and adequate psychology and the various determinations have been exhausted. Such a writer will be interested in what we don't understand rather than in what we do. He will be interested in possibility rather than probability. He will be interested in characters who are forced out to meet evil and grace and who act on a trust beyond themselves—whether they know very clearly what it is they act upon or not. To the modern mind, this kind of character, and his creator, are typical Don Quixotes, tilting at what is not there.[5]

This kind of storyteller, O'Connor surmises, "will use the concrete in a more drastic way. His way will much more obviously be *the way of distortion*."[6] As an admirer of O'Connor's fiction and biblical Hebrew storytelling, I have been struck at how O'Connor's description of Southern gothic writers also captures so well ancient biblical Hebrew storytellers. In the older testament, and particularly in the Pentateuch, we find stories that lean into this way of distortion, at least to our modern taste. In this chapter, I want to explore the way the disfigured, slant, and grotesque makes use of the concrete world to point to the mysterious working of God in the world. This exploration may also help to account for the more scandalous or shocking elements of biblical storytelling as a way of offering us an invitation to go deeper into the story rather than feeling alienated from it.

Grotesque Vignettes in the Pentateuch

Let's begin with a brief and possibly familiar occurrence: As part of a new year's resolution, a person commits to reading through the entire Bible in a year. They find a helpful daily guide to reading online and begin with Genesis. Feeling encouraged, the first days turn to weeks as they travel through the exodus with Moses. The reader, spurred on by their forward momentum, pushes through the second half of Exodus, a bit bored but motivated as they read about the detailed instructions for the tent of meeting and the exacting production of it, down to exact cubit and thread counts. Then, one morning, they open to Leviticus 1. The presence of gore

5. O'Connor, *Mystery and Manners*, 41–42.
6. O'Connor, *Mystery and Manners*, 42 (italics added).

confronts the reader within the first verses, with language of slaughter, blood flung against altar and tent walls, body parts arranged in pieces, and fat sizzling over a fire. The reader is overwhelmed and a bit put off. And there is no respite. Leviticus continues, sometimes mundane and often blood-soaked, to describe bled-out animals and dismemberment. Later in the book, the reader will come to descriptions of the human experience, with lavish details on bodily fluids and diseases. Discussion of menstruation, semen, and oozing sores is not exactly fodder for morning devotional material. The person's new year's resolution fades not too long after the commitment to regular gym visits or the keeping of gratitude journals. Leviticus makes the grotesque unavoidable and the task of reading through the Bible seemingly insurmountable.

While Leviticus is a book saturated with gore, the grotesque *does* appear in earlier stories of the Pentateuch and continues to show up through to the newer testament. Leviticus simply lays bare the grotesque elements sprinkled throughout Scripture. The bloody, violent, and bodily disfiguring are not there for entertainment value; instead (as O'Connor astutely observes), these features serve to push readers to the very edge of concrete expression in order to help us infer God at work in the world. Leviticus, I think, is arguably the most theological of the Pentateuch books, maybe of the entire older testament, because it drives so unrelentingly into the threshold space where the human and created world touches the divine.

As an Episcopalian, I am brought into the realm of the grotesque each time I receive the Eucharist: "the blood of Christ, the cup of salvation."[7] This language of blood, of gore, follows the spirit of the priestly tradition found in Leviticus. In other places in the Pentateuch we also find the grotesque at work in less extensive but still pointed and startling ways. Sometimes we see this feature in relation to a character's own body, other times in relation to a secondary character's, and still other times, as with a theophany, when someone meets God face to face.

Theologian and priest Katherine Sonderegger captures brilliantly how attending to the stories of Scripture—including and perhaps most especially those that are more uncomfortable for the modern reader—is an important theological task. In the book of Leviticus, she argues, we find

7. *Book of Common Prayer* (1979), 365.

that the "Divine Mystery is *laid down* in the sinews of the text, quietly and radically suffusing the whole, illuminating the whole with an alien Light, an astonishment and a Herald from afar."[8] Sonderegger describes something akin to what O'Connor describes as the way of distortion. What they are both describing is something that stands outside of time, place, and any kind of limit, and yet it breaks into the created world. Often this "alien Light" shows up by way of the "indirect, contrastive, unexpected Manifestation of Divine Reality," which Sonderegger describes as "simmer[ing] in every corner of Holy Scripture, even in the dark ones, graciously there."[9] This evocative language of divine disclosure as luminous, even in the darkest corners of biblical narrative, discloses how the scandalous and grotesque can also be an invitation to find grace, God's presence, unusually and inexplicably at work in the world. The idea here echoes what we see in the characterization of God in Exodus. The hiddenness of God is also a kind of revelation; saying little sometimes suggests a lot. In the life of the human being, individually and communally, we find these dark shadows also serving as opportunities for theological reflection and possibly divine disclosure.

The Grotesque in Relation to an Individual Body

Arguably, one of the more grotesque descriptions in the Pentateuch is also one of the most unassuming. In Genesis 17, the act of circumcision is instituted as a sign of the covenant God has made with Abraham. We are told that all male members of Abraham's household over eight days old must be circumcised, including servants and slaves (Gen. 17:9–14). The verb form used here for "be circumcised" is plural reflexive, meaning that from this verb form, we can infer that the community is meant to circumcise one another.

The description does not assume that the meaning of God's instructions was clear to Abraham and his household. They are explicitly commanded to circumcise *the flesh of their foreskins*. This phrase, "flesh of foreskin," appears no less than five times in Genesis 17. I highlight this repetition to point out that this passage does not mirror our modern sensibilities. Sure, Abraham needed to know the specifics of what precisely was to be

8. Sonderegger, *Doctrine of the Holy Trinity*, 381 (italics original).
9. Sonderegger, *Doctrine of the Holy Trinity*, 381.

circumcised, but why repeat the details so many times? Wasn't it obvious after the first time what was meant to be cut? (Kind of hard to forget, right?) The narrator seems to find it important to reiterate the point, that the flesh that covers the tip of a man's penis is to be removed. A number of practical and metaphorical reasons have been offered for why the act is to be taken up by Abraham and his descendants—from issues of cleanliness to wounding the mark of manliness. Whatever the conclusion reached, it seems worth noting that this description in all its detail recurs to the point of redundancy.

Not only are we given the detailed anatomy involved in the procedure, but we are told that all men over eight days old in Abraham's household were circumcised, including Abraham at the ripe age of ninety-nine years. Here we find an image of an older, mature man removing the foreskin of his penis with a knife. You can find memorable images from the medieval era that capture this scene. A quick online search will uncover a number of artistic renderings, including a rather detailed image from a fourteenth-century English Bible that shows Abraham with his legs spread open and his genitals on full display as another man takes a knife to the tip of Abraham's penis. Amusingly, other figures in the depiction have varied expressions ranging from interest to distress. Abraham, for his part, takes in the scene with a rather stoic dignity and very little modesty.

I do not mean to make a mere spectacle of this covenantal action. But it does seem rather spectacular, doesn't it? The image of a group of men gathered together to remove a flap of skin from their male extremities. The spectacle keeps us attending to the concrete action of this covenant signifier. As Walter Brueggemann observes, "Circumcision as a liturgic act gives important concrete signification to a theological affirmation. . . . The signifier has a role in the thing signified. Biblical faith is never cerebral. It is always lived and acted."[10] This gruesome act is tied up in a profound and new concrete identity for Abraham and his household. Earlier, Abraham cuts up animals as part of the covenant-making ceremony with God. Now, the act of circumcision makes clear that human flesh also must be cut.[11] This radical action reflects a radical demand, not only of the mind, but of the body.

10. Brueggemann, *Genesis*, 155.
11. Alter, *Five Books of Moses*, 82n10.

The Grotesque in Relation to Another Body

The story of the binding of Isaac in Genesis 22 is one of the most remarkable stories in the Pentateuch. The pacing of the story leads readers matter-of-factly through a disturbing series of events that resolve with a last-minute appearance of a messenger of God and a reversal of fortune for Isaac. The binding of Isaac is one of the places where the presence of the *wayyiqtol*, which we explored in chapter 3, helps us to see the startling nature of the event with more clarity. Genesis 22:1–10, translated straightforwardly with the *wayyiqtol* indicated by "AND," reads as follows:

1AND it was after these things, and God tested Abraham
AND he said to him: "Abraham"
AND he said: "Here I am."
2AND he said: "Take now your son, your only one, whom you love, Isaac, and go to the land of Moriah and offer him there as a burnt offering on one of the mountains, which I will tell to you."
3AND Abraham arose early in the morning
AND he saddled his donkey
AND he took two of his servants with him and Isaac his son
AND he split wood for a burnt offering
AND he arose
AND he went to the place which God spoke to him.
4AND (on the third day) Abraham lifted his eyes
AND he saw the place from afar.
5AND Abraham said to his servants: "Remain here with the donkey, and I and the boy will go over there and we will worship and we will return to you."
6AND Abraham took the wood of the burnt offering
AND he laid it upon Isaac his son
AND he took in his hand the fire and the knife
AND they both went on together.
7AND Isaac said to Abraham his father
AND he said: "My father"
AND he said: "Here I am my son"
AND he said: "Look! The fire and the wood and where is the lamb for the burnt offering?"
8AND Abraham said: "God will find for himself the lamb for the burnt offering my son"
AND they both went on together.

9AND they came to the place which God spoke to him
AND Abraham built the altar there
AND he arranged the wood
AND he bound Isaac his son
AND he set him upon the altar on top of the wood.
10AND Abraham stretched out his hand
AND he took the knife in order to slaughter his son.

And then, at the last moment, the sacrificial ceremony is interrupted and halted by a divine messenger who bursts onto the scene calling Abraham's name (v. 11), telling him not to use his outstretched hand to kill his son (v. 12) and providing an alternative creature to slaughter (v. 13).

Far from elegant, my translation of this event's rising action leading into the climactic appearance of the angel offers us a sharp view of the shocking spectacle of this narrative. A number of narrative features alert us as readers to the grotesque nature of this unfolding story. I want to focus on two: (1) the disparity in pacing and subject matter and (2) the function of possessives to heighten the scene.

First, the narrative plods along at an almost tedious pace. This story would be a rather boring one in its first half if we didn't have the ominously designated creature of the sacrifice. The narrator characterizes Abraham as obedient to God through the presence of the command/fulfillment formula. God tells Abraham to take his son, go to a specific land, and offer his son as a burnt offering in the place that God will show him. We read in the following verses how Abraham does just that. He gets up early in the morning and prepares for the journey. He gathers those who will accompany him, saddles his donkey, splits wood for the fire, and travels along until he arrives at the place that God will show him. Upon finding said place, he efficiently takes only what he needs (the sacrifice, the split wood, and his knife) and prepares an altar, lays wood upon it, binds up the sacrifice upon the wood, and prepares to slit the sacrifice's throat and light the sacrificial fire. The rather glaring reality that the sacrifice is his son functions to unsettle the reader. This is a reality particularly unsettling because the alarming nature of the sacrifice sits in stark relief to an otherwise quotidian story. This unsettling effect reminds me of a scary movie where everything suggests a prosaic scene, except for, say, the music or a dark shadowed corner. The way the story plods along makes the extraordinary content of the story all the more incongruous.

Second, the details of this spare story demand that readers attend to the fact that Abraham's intended sacrifice is his son, his only son, whom he loves. The short dialogue we find at the heart of this story (Gen. 22:7–8) emphasizes this perverse setup for sacrifice. The narrator tells us that Isaac speaks to *his* father, and Isaac in dialogue reiterates this idea by saying "*my* father." Many translations skip over this redundancy, collapsing the two clauses into one, or only including one of the two possessives present in Isaac speaking to "*his* father"/"*my* father." Additionally, Abraham's response similarly echoes this language of possession, where in both verse 7 and verse 8 Abraham responds to Isaac as "*my* son." These designations overtly heighten the tension that leads to the climactic moment of disruption by the angel in Genesis 22:11. But they also startle us as readers. The possessives put front and center the reality of what is being asked of Abraham. They force us to either confront the absurd situation in which Abraham finds himself or dismiss it as an empty divine command. As Abraham travels for three days alongside his son, he knows that eventually he will end up binding together his son's hands and feet to make easy access to the slitting of his throat. The standard sacrificial language coupled with the intensely personal possessives "*my* father" and "*my* son" functions in a disturbing and highly evocative way.

The use of pacing and the possessive in Genesis 22 creates a haunting effect for readers. Muted by the seeming ordinary nature of the journey, the undeniably macabre reality of a father offering his son as a sacrifice results in a troubling and evocative invitation to readers. It is no wonder that this story has become one of the most recognizable in art and literature.

The Grotesque in Relation to God

In chapter 3, we saw how Jacob wrestling with the angel-man in Genesis 32 serves as an archetypal case of biblical Hebrew narrative pacing. In addition to its pacing, this story offers us a place where we see a wounding, a rather grotesque wounding, by God (here God's messenger) as the wrestling match nears daybreak. Many of the artistic depictions of this wrangling match appear almost ethereal, like the painting by Gustave Moreau in the nineteenth century (see fig. 6.1).

In Moreau's image, the angel seems entirely unconcerned with a truly physical altercation with Jacob. Jacob and the angel in fact don't appear to touch; instead, we see only hints that the angel's foot *may* strike Jacob's leg or its hand touch Jacob's arm. The Hebrew narrative, on the other hand, offers us an acutely entangled and physical scene, particularly in Genesis 32:25, where we read of Jacob being injured as the day breaks. The verb used here for when the angel touches Jacob's hip is generally translated as "to touch" or "to strike." English translations tend to translate this action as a striking movement. Though this is not a gentle description, it also does not fully capture the violence of the strike. In striking Jacob's hip (literally translated as "the hollow of his hip"), the angel injures Jacob severely enough to not only hurt him in the moment but disable him for the rest of his life.

The Hebrew offers us a hint that this is no normal strike with the inclusion of a preposition that homes in on what is struck: "and he struck him *in* the hollow of his hip" (Gen. 32:25). This language of a focused strike (the "to strike" verb paired with a preposition indicating the object struck) appears throughout the Old Testament. As one example, we see this same construct in 1 Samuel 6:9 when the Israelites are warned about God's punishment if they mishandle the ark of the covenant. Another example is found in Job 1:19 with the description of the windstorm that collapses Job's home. Before we are told of the extent of the injury, we already see hints of the violent action wrought on Jacob. The language is meant to make us flinch. This injury is one that hurts.

Figure 6.1. *Jacob and the Angel*, by Gustave Moreau, ca. 1870.

Jacob's physical injury is further drawn out by the second half of Genesis 32:25, with the dislocation of his hip. Notably, the same verb root used here to signal dislocation can also be used to speak of someone looking away in disgust. This linking of dislocation and disgust is likely unsurprising for anyone who has ever seen a dislocation. Even a smaller dislocation, like a dislocated finger, is enough to make for a queasy stomach (as an aside, in my early twenties I dislocated a finger and sat in an emergency waiting room with a paper towel unceremoniously draped over my hand to try to keep others in the waiting room from feeling sick). In verse 35, we have a *large* dislocation of the strongest joint in the body. A common hip injury involving the sciatic nerve makes a simple action, like walking, painful, even unbearable. In the Jewish tradition, this common injury is often identified with Jacob's limp.[12] The sciatic nerve connects the spinal cord with the muscles in the legs and feet. Anyone who has had a lower back injury likely knows that in diagnosing the injury, sciatic nerve pinching can be indicated by intense pain and numbness down into the legs and feet. Even pressure that doesn't cause long-term injury (as is the case in women who experience sciatica late in their pregnancy as pelvic muscles relax in preparation for labor) can make normal daily routines uncomfortable, even impossible for a time. All to say, Jacob's injury here at the hands of an angel is a serious sort. Far from Moreau's depiction, biblical narrative gives us a rather grisly depiction of God's touch.

Attending to the extent of Jacob's wounding places the blessing he receives in a particular sort of light. This blessing is not cheap and easy. It costs Jacob something. That cost includes a limp, but it also invites us as readers to wonder about how this wounding might have impacted Jacob in areas of his life that are not so evident. A clever, creative, and cunning young man experiences a wound that he cannot remedy. A gruesome injury offers him something new—a new view of himself and of God—that accompanies the blessing marked by a new name.

The Pentateuch contains many more examples of the grotesque, the unsettling, and the scandalous. For example, the children's Bible story of the ark is a far cry from the narrative description we find of the flood in Genesis 7–8. Embedded in that story is an invitation to take the scenic view of the flood, peering out from the ark to see the devastation and death-filled waters around; more, imagine the sight as God brought a strong wind across the land to make the water recede. There are also stories of

12. Sarna, *JPS Torah Commentary: Genesis*, 228.

sexual violence, particularly in Genesis, that should unsettle us as readers and invite us to wonder what is going on here. Not to ignore the presence of sexual violence and not to excuse it but to wrestle with the bits of Scripture that unsettle us and make for a spectacle. For the remainder of this chapter, though, I want to focus on a story in the book of Numbers that could be adapted well as a modern-day horror story as the land itself splits open and brings people with eyes wide open into the realm of death.

Case Study: Numbers 16

Numbers may best be understood as a patchwork of material concerning the important stories and family lines that mark the two wilderness generations: the older generation liberated from enslavement in Egypt and the younger generation who will put down roots in the promised land. Within the book, we receive intimate pictures of life in the wilderness through vignettes of Moses and Aaron's struggle to lead a weary and disillusioned people through their wilderness wanderings. One of the most extravagant and haunting of these stories involves a member of Moses and Aaron's own tribe, Korah the Levite, questioning the legitimacy of Moses and Aaron's leadership.

We pick up the story in Numbers 16:1 with Korah and two other Israelites, Dathan and Abiram from the tribe of Reuben, leading a group of prominent Israelites to confront Moses and Aaron. This group, numbering over 250 men, insists collectively that Moses and Aaron are overreaching regarding their authority over the rest of the Israelites. They argue that this community should be egalitarian, recognizing that all of the Israelites are holy, that God is with all of them, and that no one should be exalted over another (16:3).

The presence of rebellion against Moses and Aaron's leadership is not new in Numbers. Earlier, in Numbers 11–14, a series of stories unfold that are marked by lamenting and questioning Moses's leadership—including complaints by Moses's own siblings, Aaron and Miriam. This story, despite its dramatic resolution, will also not be the last of the rebellions. Later, we find *all* the Israelites rebelling against these two brothers (16:41–50). So what we find in the story of Korah's rebellion is not unique in theme but is simply the most extravagant of judgments by God amid an unceasingly complaining people.

Before getting to the heart of this chilling scene of judgment, let us spend a moment looking to Korah and his complaint. Korah is not an insignificant figure. His name is included in Exodus 6 as a member in the list of ancestral families before liberation from Egypt. Among the Levites, Korah's uncle is Moses and Aaron's father. With Moses and Aaron as the leaders of the wandering Israelites, Korah stands not only as a member of the special line of the Levites but as a close family member, a cousin, of the community's highest leaders. Korah is accompanied by two named Reubenite leaders, plus 250 other unnamed prominent leaders. These leaders are designated with a title that can also be translated as "chieftains" or "princes"; that is to say, this is not simply a riotous mob coming to complain to leadership but a group of distinguished leaders from among the congregation. I point this out simply to highlight the possibly disingenuous call for "all people" to be set apart and designated holy. A large group of ordinary folks calling for equality rings, at least for me, a bit more true than a large group of distinguished leaders making that same call. The fact that the two people who accompany Korah are from the tribe of Reuben strengthens the possibility that this call for equality is disingenuous. In Numbers 1–2, we read about a change in the accounting for the ancestral houses: in the first chapter, the Reubenites are listed first, whereas in the next listing they are displaced by the tribe of Judah. One commentator captures this shift as a clear demotion in rank for the Reubenites among the tribes, adding that not only has the tribal order changed but also the diminished numbers of the Reuben tribe in Numbers 2 are mirrored by the increased numbers among those in the Judah clan.[13] This demotion in status offers us a hint at why these two Reubenites are leading the charge with Korah; it's possible that these are less than loyal figures and that the narrator is offering us a subtle hint that characterizes this group of leaders as possessing ulterior motives.

Let us return to the unfolding events in Numbers 16. Moses responds to the complaint of Korah and his associates by falling on his face, language that offers readers a picture of Moses on his knees or even stomach, with his face to the ground (v. 4). This posture seems a bit odd to us, but Moses finds himself with his face in the dirt a number of times in the wilderness journey, including two more times in this chapter in verses 22 and 45, these times accompanied by Aaron. The recurrence of this posture for Moses is

13. Olson, *Numbers*, 103.

tied to the act of intercessory prayer; most frequently Moses and Aaron are interceding on behalf of the Israelites and trying to serve as a buffer of sorts between God and the people. In Numbers 16:4 we do not read of any appeal Moses makes to God, but that appeal is implied by the fact that Moses's next words are to Korah and contain instructions about God's decision regarding their complaint. Moses here relays a message he received from God that is not shared with the readers.

Moses tells Korah and his associates that God will clarify who is holy and who can approach God (Num. 16:5). As part of Moses's response, we already see a refutation of the call for equality, which likely gets to the heart of the issue (a desire for someone other than Moses and Aaron to be the leader of Israel): "Do this: take censers, Korah and all your company, and tomorrow put fire in them, and lay incense on them before the LORD; and *the man whom the LORD chooses shall be the holy one*. You Levites have gone too far!" (16:6–7 NRSV). Moses's proclamation cutting to the heart of the issue is further exposed in the chastisement that follows, as Moses calls out the Levites for not being satisfied with already being set apart as the chosen tribe to serve in the tent of meeting (16:9–10).

There is a lot happening in these verses that contain Moses's rebuke. One commentator organizes Moses's response into six parts, helpfully mapping the many statements that appear in Numbers 16:4–17:

1. Moses's intercession notes that the questioning of Moses and Aaron's leadership is in fact an attack on God's choice in leaders (v. 4).
2. Moses invites Korah and his crew to come to the tent of meeting in the morning with instructions on censers (vv. 5–8).
3. Moses complains pointedly against Korah and Korah's dissatisfaction with the special work God has already given them of looking after the tabernacle and ministering to the people (vv. 8–11).
4. Moses requests to speak with Dathan and Abiram, which the two men ignore, preferring to grumble among themselves (vv. 12–14).
5. Moses grows incredibly angry and defends his own actions and innocence before God (v. 15).
6. The final response reiterates the early instructions to Korah and his crew, setting the stage for the next morning (vv. 16–17).[14]

14. Olson, *Numbers*, 103–4.

While we do not know what all occurred in Moses's intercession with God at the start of his response to the rebels' complaint, we can surmise from this sequence that neither Moses nor God is happy with the company's complaints and that something big is coming in the morning, which is signaled by the repetition of instructions about how to prepare for it.

Characteristic of the brevity of biblical Hebrew narrative, the pacing moves us along to the next morning without any temporal indication. Numbers 16:16–17 repeats the instructions for the next morning. Then verse 18 begins, and the next morning is abruptly upon us as all are present before the tent of meeting. Just as suddenly, in verse 19 the glory of God appears before Korah and all present. The pacing does not slow as the next verse outlines God's instruction to Moses and Aaron to step away from all those present, "so that I may consume them in a moment" (16:20 NRSV). Or, as Eugene Peterson puts it in *The Message*: "So that I can finish them off and be done with them." In response, we find Moses once again with his face to the ground, this time accompanied by Aaron, asking God not to punish a whole group of people for one man's waywardness. God hears their plea and asks for not only Moses and Aaron but all those present to get away from the lodgings of Korah, Dathan, and Abiram, for something very, very bad is about to happen to them that will make clear that God, and not Moses, has made the decision of leadership among the Israelites.

All present, besides the families of Korah, Dathan, and Abiram, clear out from all the surrounding area of these three men's camps. Moses then declares: "This is how you shall know that the Lord has sent me to do all these works; it has not been of my own accord: If these people die a natural death, or if a natural fate comes on them, then the Lord has not sent me. But if the Lord creates something new, and the ground opens its mouth and swallows them up, with all that belongs to them, and they go down alive into Sheol, then you shall know that these men have despised the Lord" (Num. 16:28–30 NRSV). Moses prepares both the onlookers and the rebels for how to interpret the events that immediately follow his proclamation. Lest anyone think that Moses is a liar or misrepresenting God's chosen leadership, what the people are about to see is a judgment that only God, and not a human, can accomplish. What they are about to see cannot be mistaken as a natural disaster; this disaster is a divine one.

Remember, these people are already well acquainted with divine action breaking into the world through plagues, the parting of a sea, and the appearance of miraculous food and springs of water. I imagine, though, that this description of events about to unfold was more terrifying and awe-inspiring than these prior events because here God is not the great liberator from oppression and provider in the wilderness but judge of all, including the Israelite among Israelites (which foreshadows the judgment of Achan and his clan later in Josh. 7). They know the power of God, but here they see the power of God at work against insiders, a faction of God's chosen people.

God's actions not only display power in judgment but use grotesque action to assure this image sticks in the minds of those who look on. To go down alive into Sheol is not simply violent or theatrical; it captures the heart of the grotesque as making strange and perverse the ways the world usually works. This act of going into the realm of the dead alive is a challenge to the usual way of things, to the knowledge that the realm of the dead is for the dead, in the same way that the realm of the living is for those alive. This judgment is a kind of reverse zombie apocalypse: rather than the dead acting alive among the living, the alive enter into the realm of the dead still alive.

In Numbers 16:32–33, God shows both his affirmation of Moses's leadership and his judgment of the rebels as God creates "something new," something grotesque: the earth splits open, and the rebels descend fully alive into the realm of the dead, along with all their possessions. Just as suddenly as the earth splits open, the ground covers them up, possibly muffling cries of terror as they descend below the ground.

Much like the story that comes later in the book of Joshua about the judgment of Achan (Josh. 7), the demise here in Numbers 16 is especially disturbing because not only the rebels but their entire families are punished. We are told that Korah, Dathan, and Abiram stood outside their tents with their entire families—wives, sons, and little ones—waiting on God's judgment (Num. 16:27). The reference to these three distinct groups heightens the horror of the event. And then the men's entire households are swallowed up with them as the ground opens up. The little ones and the elders are together pulled down into the realm of the dead still alive. The mention of "little ones" is unusual. For instance, in a similar story of the destruction of Achan's household, Achan's household includes his sons and daughters, but there is no additional inference of toddlers. I wonder if this mention suggests that these were grandchildren in order to demonstrate that three generations of their family were wiped out. Or maybe the mention is meant to emphasize the absolutely grotesque judgment of action to follow, painting a picture for the reader of not only adults but small children disappearing alive into the realm of the dead.

God's judgment doesn't end here, with the splitting of the earth and the demise of the central leaders. We are told that after the rebels and their households vanished, a fire like the one that consumed Nadab and Abihu in Leviticus lashes out and consumes 250 men, presumably the same men that opened this scene at the start of the chapter. Both in a new way and in a familiar way, God shows his judgment by doing what only a creator God can do—splitting earth asunder and raining down fire from the heavens.

It is hard to read this story as one of mercy, though it is that. God does spare the entire congregation after Moses and Aaron intercede on their behalf in Numbers 16:20–22. It is also hard to read this story as one of discernment, though it is also that. The discernment of true leadership comes about by God directly showing who the true leaders are among the Israelites. If nothing else, one hopes that this extreme judgment and disclosure of God's chosen leaders would confirm among the wandering people the validity of their leaders and the demand to fall in line with them. But, alas, we are told that the morning after this event the entire congregation rebels against Moses and Aaron (16:41).

So how are we to read this story? It is so full of violence, and it appears to have little effect on the people who watched the horrific scene unfold. I think a start to engaging a story like this one is to return to Flannery O'Connor's conviction that to engage stories like this, we as readers need to have a "whole view of things." In this case, a "whole view" includes understanding what is at stake in this moment. Moses and Aaron are leading a newly liberated and vulnerable people into the land God promised them. This journey has already been drastically sidelined when God realizes that they need to wander a generation longer before they can enter this land, with the possibility of their remaining a faithful and distinct people as part of the Abrahamic promise. God speaks to Moses, directly to Moses, more than God speaks directly to anyone else in the Old Testament. Moses as God's prophet and chosen leader is the means by which God guides ancient Israel into a land of their own. Joshua's designation later as the "new Moses" only solidifies the centrality of Moses's role in the wilderness. Moses's leadership is key to God's plan for the wandering

Israelites. This whole view of things does not excuse or ignore this grotesque story, with reverse zombies and little ones falling through cracks in the ground. Instead, it offers readers the context in which to wrestle with our discomfort, something to guide our disgust, our fear, and our questions through a text like this one.

Conclusion

While not resolving the discomfort of the grotesque aspects in the Pentateuch, I hope this chapter helps you to garner an appreciation for the ways that the macabre and scandalous can draw readers more deeply into the possibility of God at work in the world. As Sonderegger so aptly characterizes it, God shows up "simmering in every corner of Holy Scripture, even in the dark ones, graciously there."[15] The God we find in the Pentateuch does not stand at a distance, disinterested or disgusted with the very material aspects of being human. God communes with ancient Israel in the everyday realities of being human—bodily fluids, foreskins, and all. At the same time, God works within the world to make clear that God, not influential figures or competing gods, has mastery over the created order. These two aspects—God working through the grotesquely mundane and with fear-inducing power—capture the reality that God has made a dwelling place among the people, as the God who draws near in flame and cloud and as the God who stands apart as Creator of all things.

15. Sonderegger, *Doctrine of the Holy Trinity*, 381.

CHAPTER 7

Deuteronomy, Eat These Stories

Introduction

In book 3 of *The Republic*, Socrates concerns himself with the poets in his discussion on forming the best and brightest young people in his perfect city. He spends a good amount of this book speaking to his brother Adeimantus about the importance of telling certain kinds of stories (those about heroes and the gods in the early education of the city's future leaders) and avoiding others, because stories hold power and are more than fanciful forms of entertainment. Stories are models of virtue (or vice), opportunities for imitation in the way of justice—or injustice, if the wrong stories are told. Stories are pedagogical; they form their readers even if readers are unaware of their effect. Thus Socrates argues for censorship of the stories told to these young leaders. Many of us bristle at the word "censorship," but I would guess we would also agree that certain stories are not meant for all ages and that some stories simply should not be told at all. Whether we are fully cognizant of it or not, we all innately know this truth: stories matter. They shape how we view ourselves and our world.

The stories we find in the Bible are stories that have been passed down and reworked into the final form we now have. Much of the energy among biblical scholars in the late nineteenth century and into the twentieth century focused on pulling back the layers of the final form of a text to find the oldest stories that served as the kernel, the center, of the stories that other texts came to surround. These investigations are fascinating because they help us thousands of years later to imagine how generation after generation received, reshaped, and passed on the biblical narratives. The word "tradition" finds its roots in the ways that stories (and beliefs) are passed down from one generation to another, with its etymological roots in the Latin word *tradere* (to trade, hand down). This work of revising and adding to stories also tells us something about what stories do. Like Socrates's preferred poets, the narratives of the Bible (especially the early stories in the Pentateuch) serve as pivotal formative stories for the nation of ancient Israel and for the Christian church, which has been grafted into ancient Israel.

Deuteronomy and Remembrance

No book quite captures the importance of stories being told and retold to future generations like the book of Deuteronomy. In this book, an older generation, represented by Moses, tells the younger generation, including Moses's successor, Joshua, the summation of the most important stories of Hebrew identity as the promised land looms in the distant horizon. As Moses begins his address, he does not set out to rehearse verbatim the same story once again but to *retell* it in such a way as to contextualize the past story of God and God's actions for this people in light of the present moment for those he addresses. That is, this telling goes beyond replicating stories of the past. The story of God told throughout the books of Genesis, Exodus, Leviticus, and Numbers is an invitation into an unfolding drama—a story of yesterday, today, and tomorrow.

In his introduction to Old Testament theology, W. H. Bellinger speaks of the way a "curated memory" functions within the legal material of the Old Testament alongside the abundance of narrative to provide a lens through which the generations that follow understand themselves and their ethical mandate in the world.[1] The language of curation reminds me of Socrates's emphasis on censorship. Not just any memory will do here. The memory of what God has done in and through the patriarchs, matriarchs, and their descendants recalls the God who seeks to be in their midst. The stories preserved in the first four books of the Pentateuch and reframed in Deuteronomy are not just any stories told in any kind of way; instead,

1. Bellinger, *Introducing Old Testament Theology*, 14.

they have been shaped in such a way as to be passed on and adopted anew in subsequent generations. These origin stories of God's love, favor, mercy, and call for obedience reverberate throughout the whole of the older testament and into the revelation of God in Jesus in the newer testament.

Bellinger identifies this construction of a curated memory as functioning not only in the life of the ancients but as ongoing in the life of faithful readers:

> People view reality through constructs that guide the perception and interpretation of experience. . . . These constructs become part of our memory, shaping how we live and how we view life. And we test these constructs in our experience. These constructs can lead to the social construction of our reality and to important questions about power and social location involved in our hermeneutical work on the Older Testament. By way of these constructs, these ancient texts wield authority in liturgical communities. Narrative and memory are central in the appropriation of Old Testament theology in the life of faith.[2]

The invitation of reading is not simply an invitation to dive back into stories of the past. Stories invite us—like the hearers of Moses's final addresses in Deuteronomy—to envision our own lives and expressions of faith in the present through the work of remembering what God has already done. Recollecting faith stories gives us an identity in our present moment and a vision for the future. As Bellinger aptly summarizes, "Memory focuses both the present and the future."[3]

At the start of Deuteronomy we find not a narrative but rather a narrative summary. For the first three chapters, Moses recalls the places, events, and trials of the wilderness wanderings and ends with God's refusal to permit Moses to enter into the land of promise. This rehearsal of events serves as the foundation on which Moses gives his final instructions before the Israelites will enter the land, without him. While the text itself can seem redundant at times, what we find here is not a copy-and-paste job but a fresh reception of foundational stories of identity. Gerhard von Rad captures this idea of reception aptly in his introduction to Deuteronomy, as he reflects on those who compiled the book into its final form: "How

2. Bellinger, *Introducing Old Testament Theology*, 14.
3. Bellinger, *Introducing Old Testament Theology*, 14.

enduring and valid the ancient tradition appeared to these preachers is evident from the fact that they like to adduce not indeed 'proof texts' but yet a *proof from tradition*. Not only the legal traditions but historical events, too, have significance as a standard for the present day of the preacher."[4] Von Rad draws out a fact that may seem obvious to us as modern readers, yet it is not always credited intertextually as well: the stories and legislations of the early biblical traditions remain important for subsequent generations. The generation preparing to enter the promised land receives a good reminder from Moses, much like a good Sunday morning sermon reminds us that Jesus's call to the disciples in first-century Palestine is also a call to us (and to the generations that came between then and now). The idea of "a proof from tradition" draws out how important it is to return again and again to biblical narratives not as historical documents to be studied from a distance but as testimonies of God's work in the world that are to be read, learned, and inwardly digested in this present moment.

Stories as Vehicles for Identity

Remembrance plays a key role in the larger book of Deuteronomy. The verb "to remember" is central for understanding the identity of the Israelites, thus the persistent refrain of the promise to Abraham, Isaac, and Jacob throughout the older testament. But, in Deuteronomy, this call to remember takes on a heightened pitch. Over a third of all the calls to remember in the Pentateuch appear here in its final book, with a call for ancient Israel to remember how far God has taken them as they prepare to set foot in the promised land. This call to remembrance is heightened with the insistence that this recollection not remain with the present generation but continue on to this generation's "children and children's children" (Deut. 4:9; 6:2).

In Deuteronomy, the call to remembrance is not only a list of mandates for life together that echoes the Holiness Code in Leviticus, though the latter half of Deuteronomy does include hefty portions of this kind of material. Neither does the call to remembrance simply reiterate the Ten Commandments, though we do find those central commands in Deuteronomy 5:6–21. What we find in Deuteronomy is a lengthy rehearsal, sometimes

4. Von Rad, *Deuteronomy*, 20 (italics added).

ad nauseum, of how God worked in, through, and for Abraham, Isaac, Jacob, and their descendants so that they could be faithful witnesses to the whole world. Retelling and recasting these stories frames and orients the mandates about how these people are to live in the promised land with the God of Israel as their one true God. Like Socrates, Moses recognizes the importance of the stories we tell because they give shape to both identity and moral action.

At the heart of this remembrance is Deuteronomy 6, which contains the Shema, a prayer that remains at the core of Jewish identity to this day: "Hear, O Israel: The Lord is our God, the Lord alone" (Deut. 6:4 NRSV). In this pivotal chapter, Moses unfurls a series of instructions for ancient Israel to remember so that it may go well for them in the new land:

- Listen! God is one and deserving of all your love (vv. 4–5).
- Do not forget what you are told today (v. 6).
- Repeat these commands to your children (v. 7a).
- Talk about them all the time, day and night (v. 7b).
- Affix them on your bodies (v. 8).
- Write them at the entrance to your homes (v. 9).
- Do not forget that God liberated you from enslavement when you enter the land and things are going well (vv. 10–12).
- Fear God (v. 13).
- Do not test God as you once did (v. 16).
- Do what is right before God (v. 18).
- Tell the stories of what God has done for us when your children ask why we live as we do (vv. 20–25).

The call to remember has a theological foundation: God is one, not many; God is worthy of all love, fear, and obedience; and God has been made known in history through miraculous and liberating actions in the life of the patriarchs and their descendants. Stories serve as the vehicle by which the Israelites are to remember and to educate future generations.

Storytelling is a common practice across cultures and time. Stories serve as vehicles for identity. Telling them is a practice of educating people in where they come from and who they are today. Stories provide the framework for conviction. We see this in the desire to know our family histories, the popularity of genealogy research and family trees, the resurgence of interest in local histories, and the ways that stories of the past ground the identity of marginalized and oppressed people groups. We can even see the way stories work in theology. The connection between theological propositional claims and storied reasoning extends into the life of the early Christian church as the construction of the rule of faith (*regula fidei)* helped guide right action and right reading of Scripture. This rule was later fleshed out most robustly in the Nicene Creed. The Christian orthodox claims about who God is center on how God has been revealed in the world, with the pinnacle moment being the story of the incarnation. Stories matter. Telling and retelling stories grounds our theological and moral claims.

At the heart of Deuteronomy is a call to remember the identity of the people preparing to enter the land of promise. The recollection of identity in Deuteronomy centers on the story of the exodus and an oppressed people liberated by a loving God. Within the book of Exodus, we see an awareness of the centrality of the exodus event for future generations in the instructions for the Passover: "This day shall be a day of remembrance for you. You shall celebrate it as a festival to the Lord; throughout your generations you shall observe it as a perpetual ordinance" (Exod. 12:14 NRSV). God's liberative acts in the first half of Exodus define the identity not only of a generation freed from enslavement but of the generations that follow. The centrality of this story of liberation as identity-forming extends well past the generation that stands on the edge of the promised land in Deuteronomy. Many generations later, the exiled community recalls the same exodus story to be reminded of both who they are and how they have failed to behave as the chosen people of God.

For example, Rebecca Poe Hays identifies Psalm 78 as a psalm that speaks to people in the trauma of exile with a remembrance of both identity and judgment.[5] Psalm 78 begins with a familiar call, one we find in the early chapters of Deuteronomy: listen; remember the stories of our ancestors; do not keep them to yourself; tell future generations about God's saving acts. As the psalm unfolds the salvific work of God in the life of ancient Israel and their apostatic response leading to judgment, the exiled audience is reoriented by both a reminder of who they were

5. Hays, "Trauma, Remembrance, and Healing."

and a hope for who they might be. As Hays observes, "In the wake of remembering God's pre-trauma commitment to and provision for Israel, the affirmation that this commitment still stands holds great power for shaping how the traumatized audience will reconnect with their ongoing lives."[6] God's saving acts anchor generation upon generation of ancient Israelites to recall God's liberative work, which is rooted in God's love for them and which draws back even the most wayward to God's favor. Stories serve as the primary vehicle for shaping ancient Israel, maintaining them, and reminding them who they truly are: the ones that God loved, called, and liberated.

Eat These Stories

In Eugene Peterson's *Eat This Book: A Conversation in the Art of Spiritual Reading*, he uses the image of his dog gnawing away on a bone as a fitting object lesson for the idea of truly relishing Scripture.[7] His dog's delight in a bone reminded Peterson of John of Patmos in the book of Revelation, who is told by an angelic messenger to take and eat a scroll, which was sweet on the tongue and bitter in the stomach (Rev. 10:9–10). This later biblical image of consuming the little scroll echoes the earlier prophets Jeremiah and Ezekiel, who also feasted on texts. Peterson notes wryly that eating books is "a good diet, it would seem, for anyone who cares about reading words rightly."[8] And while Peterson does not directly reference it, I am reminded of Thomas Cranmer's admonition from *The Book of Common Prayer* that we not only read, mark, and learn but inwardly *digest* Scripture.[9]

I feel, in a way, like Moses is giving a similar kind of command to his hearers in Deuteronomy in terms of the redemptive stories of God in their midst generation after generation. He is saying to his audience, "Eat these stories." Don't let them collect dust or be forgotten. In fact, keep them before you through repetition (6:6), tell your children about them (6:7), have conversations about them day and night (6:7), and affix them physically to your bodies and at the entrance of your homes (6:8–9).

6. Hays, "Trauma, Remembrance, and Healing," 203.
7. Peterson, *Eat This Book*, 1–2.
8. Peterson, *Eat This Book*, 9.
9. "Proper 28," *Book of Common Prayer* (1979), 184.

Moses's command to ancient Israel is not purely intellectual or cultic; it is a command to keep the stories before them night and day and on their lips, on their bodies, and on the buildings they inhabit. The command is an embodied kind of recollection. Eat these stories. Breathe these stories. Touch these stories. Do not forget who you are.

Peterson captures so well the idea of reading Scripture as a spiritual and formative practice, and he offers an enriched understanding of Moses's instructions in Deuteronomy. Importantly for our study, what we find in this final book of the Pentateuch is not an anomaly but the normative claim throughout the older and newer testaments' faith communities:

> We are part of a holy community that for three thousand years and more has been formed inside and out by these words of God, words that have been heard, tasted, chewed, seen, walked. Reading Holy Scripture is totally physical. Our bodies are the means of providing our souls access to God in his revelation: eat this book. A friend reports to me that one of the early rabbis selected a different part of our bodies to make the same point; he insisted that the primary body part for taking in the word of God is not the ears but the feet. You learn God, he said, not through your ears but through your feet: follow the Rabbi.
>
> And so it is the practice of the Christian community to cultivate habits of reading that sharpen our perceptions and involve us in getting this word of God formatively within us—wanting to do it as well as the best of our ancestors, determined not to leave any of these words in a book on the shelf, like a can of baked beans stored in a cupboard. We want to work up a good appetite, join St. John and eat this book.[10]

I see a link here between Moses's aim in Deuteronomy and the idea "eat this book" as a means of cultivating good habits of reading that lead to transformation. I think we might see Moses's emphasis on stories as identity-forming and as a kind of culinary invitation: eat these stories. In Deuteronomy, a number of central stories are on the menu. Let's examine four in chronological order of events to link together the stories that are meant to be ever before and within ancient Israel so that they remember who they are as they enter the land of promise: the central identity story of the Passover, the destruction of the Egyptian

10. Peterson, *Eat This Book*, 61.

army during the exodus, the manna from the heavens, and the creation of the golden calf.

The Passover

> Observe the month of Abib by keeping the passover to the LORD your God, for in the month of Abib the LORD your God brought you out of Egypt by night. You shall offer the passover sacrifice to the LORD your God, from the flock and the herd, at the place that the LORD will choose as a dwelling for his name. You must not eat with it anything leavened. For seven days you shall eat unleavened bread with it—the bread of affliction—because you came out of the land of Egypt in great haste, so that all the days of your life you may remember the day of your departure from the land of Egypt. No leaven shall be seen with you in all your territory for seven days; and none of the meat of what you slaughter on the evening of the first day shall remain until morning. You are not permitted to offer the passover sacrifice within any of your towns that the LORD your God is giving you. But at the place that the LORD your God will choose as a dwelling for his name, only there shall you offer the passover sacrifice, in the evening at sunset, the time of day when you departed from Egypt. You shall cook it and eat it at the place that the LORD your God will choose; the next morning you may go back to your tents. For six days you shall continue to eat unleavened bread, and on the seventh day there shall be a solemn assembly for the LORD your God, when you shall do no work. (Deut. 16:1–8 NRSV)

We will spend the most time on the Passover story, because this event serves as the crux of ancient Israel's identity. Through this story, we come to know the God of Israel as the one who liberated an enslaved people from a powerful foe and brought them out of bondage through signs and miracles in order to lead them into a fertile land and make a dwelling among them. Exodus 12 tells the story of the first Passover event and the institution of the feast that would mark the final act of God's liberation of ancient Israel from enslavement through the tenth and final plague. In the Hebraic imagination, the Passover marks both the specific event when the Lord passed over the firstborn of each Israelite household marked with blood, sparing them from death, and, more broadly, Pharaoh's concession to let the Israelites go, which was followed by God bringing the Israelites out from under the yoke of slavery. The Passover is a liberation story, a story summarized again and again with the words "the LORD brought you out from the land of Egypt." This refrain appears not only in Deuteronomy but is repeated by kings, prophets, and even early Christian martyrs.

In Deuteronomy, God's liberative act is framed as one rooted in God's love for God's people. This link between God's liberation and love is on full display in Deuteronomy 7:7–8: "It was not because you were more numerous than any other people that the Lord set his heart on you and chose you—for you were the fewest of all peoples. It was because the Lord loved you and kept the oath that he swore to your ancestors, that the Lord has brought you out with a mighty hand, and redeemed you from the house of slavery, from the hand of Pharaoh king of Egypt" (NRSV). Moses wants to be sure that at this crucial moment, on the threshold of the land where they will make their home, ancient Israel knows that God's love and faithfulness, and not their impressive stature, got them to this place.

The story of liberation must remain at the center of Israelite identity going forward, so much so that they must eat it in a rather literal sense. In Deuteronomy 16, Moses instructs ancient Israel to mark their liberation from Egypt by observing the Passover with two tangible elements of recollection: Passover sacrifices and unleavened bread. On the first day of the Passover observance, at the same time of day that God liberated the enslaved Israelites, future generations are to offer a Passover sacrifice and then feast on this meal in the place where God dwells among them (16:6). This feast will be followed the next morning with another six days of continuing to eat unleavened bread. Moses informs them of the reason for this special diet: "You must not eat with it anything leavened. For seven days you shall eat unleavened bread with it—the bread of affliction—because you came out of the land of Egypt in great haste." They shall do this year after year "so that all the days of your life you may remember the day of your departure from the land of Egypt" (16:3 NRSV).

The Passover narrative ripples out into subsequent generations of this people. It remains for them a story that they must read and remember not only as a way of giving thanks for how God has provided for them in yesteryears but for the God who continues to be their God in this present age. In the Passover, ancient Israel came to know God as liberator, as emancipator from enslavement. The exodus marks this people as God's own for generation upon generation. We see the importance of this story again throughout Scripture: we see it in the children of those who were preparing to enter the promised land, in their descendants in the age of the united monarchy under David and Solomon, in the divided kingdoms in the age of the prophets, in the exiled community, and even into the New Testament era of the persecuted apostles. Let us look to a few examples to see the way this story sustains the ongoing work of God among God's people.

Both David and his son Solomon offer us magnificent prayers at crucial moments in their divinely ordered kingship. In 2 Samuel 7, David offers a prayer upon learning that, while he will not be the one to make a house for God, God will make a house for him. Without a hint of disappointment that his hope to build a permanent dwelling place was thwarted, David's prayer in 2 Samuel 7:18–29 rhetorically asks who he is that God has been so faithful to him. His prayer continues moving from the singular to the corporate as he asks, "Who is like Israel," whom you have called as your own? What follows is a recollection of what God has done in and for these people, rehearsing the stories that Moses instructed the Israelites to "eat" some five hundred years earlier: "Who is like your people, like Israel? Is there another nation on earth whose God went to redeem it as a people, and to make a name for himself, doing great and awesome things for them, by driving out before his people nations and their gods? And you established your people Israel for yourself to be your people forever; and you, O Lord, became their God" (2 Sam. 7:23–24 NRSV). The Passover story, the story of God's liberating act in defying Egyptian might (both human and divine), is the heart of ancient Israel's identity.

David's progeny Solomon continues to uphold the centrality of the Passover story as he prays to dedicate the house of God that he just built (1 Kings 8:22–53). Here we directly see the thread of the Passover story as it is woven from one generation into the next. As Solomon dedicates the temple, in arguably one of the most stunning prayers in all of Scripture, he recalls the mighty things God has done in creation and in the life of this particular people. As he closes his prayer, he notes that despite their habitual disobedience, ancient Israel continues to experience God's compassion and patience, and that God continues to hear their prayers: "For they are your people and your possession, which you brought out of Egypt from the very heart of the iron crucible" (8:51). Solomon's confidence in coming before God, supposing that God will in fact listen, rests in the Passover story of God's salvific work for an enslaved people.

Following Solomon, the era of the divided kingdoms begins with waywardness in both the northern kingdom of Israel and the southern kingdom of Judah. Both kingdoms fail miserably in maintaining their identity as the chosen people of God; they cast away the old stories for shiny new identities centered on pride, selfishness, malice, and pleasure. Both kingdoms forgot, but the northern kingdom forgot more quickly. The prophet Hosea speaks to this unruly nation as the threat of Assyrian invasion becomes an actuality. He speaks to Israel both of their impending judgment and of God's love for them even in this judgment. In Hosea 13, as the prophet expounds on the coming judgment, he also reminds them who they are by recalling the Passover story: "But I am the Lord your God since your time in the land of Egypt, and you know no god except me, and there is no savior except me" (Hosea 13:4). Hosea confirms God both as the one who defeated the Egyptians' so-called gods with the tenth plague and as the God who liberated ancient Israel, who saved the ancestors of those whom Hosea addresses. It is a reminder not only of who they were meant to be but of how far they have strayed from this identity.

The saving story of the Passover continues not only as it speaks to Israel's present moment but as it offers a message of hope for their future as a soon-to-be exiled community: they are reminded that God will not abandon them, even in judgment. The prophets pick up the story of Passover and liberation, not only as a recollection of what God has done but as the archetypal story for the restoration of the exiled remnant to the promised land.

Years after Hosea's ministry, the prophet Isaiah speaks judgment on Judah, while also rehearsing an old story in a new way. The language he uses, while not directly naming the Egyptians, would have evoked the image of liberation to all his hearers: "On that day, the Lord will lift his hand for a second time to recover the remnant of his people" (Isa. 11:11). Later, as we will see, Isaiah continues this imagery of a second liberation as he reminds them of the crossing of the Red Sea. Isaiah's prophecy of restoration for the remnant returns his hearers' imaginations to a story they already know. This story is so deep in their bones that his prophetic word, even though he is speaking of coming judgment and the remainder of only a remnant from the people, offers a trustworthy promise. The audience knew that God had done this work of liberating and gathering God's people before, and Isaiah's words signal that this foundational identity is not lost in the present moment, not even in judgment.

Jumping ahead into the New Testament era, we also find the language of Passover deliverance in the mouth of Stephen in Acts 7. Stephen, falsely accused of speaking blasphemously against Moses's teachings, comes before the Sanhedrin. He demonstrates his faithfulness to Moses's instructions by retelling in great detail the story that Moses himself rehearses in Deuteronomy. At the heart of Stephen's retelling is an account of Moses's ministry and how God used Moses to liberate Israel. Here Stephen uses this retelling to remind his hearers not only of who they were but of how quickly—both back then and now—they forget their core identity. The stories he rehearses are not only about liberation but about a liberated people's continued apostasy and refusal to have eyes to see or ears to hear the work of God in their midst. This speech leads to Stephen's martyrdom.

Despite his less-than-receptive audience, we can see in Acts 7 how Stephen recognizes the liberation that God worked among those enslaved in Egypt as the linchpin for identity, as the culmination of what was promised to Abraham. This retelling is used not as a word of comfort or reassurance but as a word of condemnation. Stephen reminds people of their identity through this story, essentially asking, "Do you not know who you are? What miraculous things God has done in your midst and for your benefit? Why squash the workings of God in this present moment? Are you just as bad as the Israelites, who complained and rebelled against the very prophet God sent to liberate them?" This indictment by Stephen ends with a direct accusation: "You stiff-necked people, uncircumcised in heart and ears, you are forever opposing the Holy Spirit, just as your ancestors used to do" (7:51 NRSV). Stephen accuses these Jewish leaders of being stiff-necked like Pharaoh, opposing the work of God in their midst and forgetting who they are.

The story of the Passover holds a central place in the feast of stories that have nourished the identity of the people of God across the ages. God as liberator serves as the crux of Israel's identity through the ages of the kings (and queens), the judgment and exile, the return of a remnant, and the great liberation from the shackles of death through the God-man, Jesus Christ. Eat this story. The other stories we now turn to complement and enrich this central, identity-forming story, adding dimension both to God's provision and to the liberated people's short memories.

The Egyptian Army Destroyed

> Remember today that it was not your children (who have not known or seen the discipline of the LORD your God), but it is you who must acknowledge his greatness, his mighty hand and his outstretched arm, his signs and his deeds that he did in Egypt to Pharaoh, the king of Egypt, and to all his land; what he did to the Egyptian army, to their horses and chariots, how he made the water of the Red Sea flow over them as they pursued you, so that the LORD has destroyed them to this day. (Deut. 11:2–4 NRSV)

In Deuteronomy 11, Moses reminds his hearers that they have seen God's power at work in ways that their children have not. They know what God did in the assault of plagues on the Egyptian Pharaoh and his gods and the destruction of the Egyptian army at the Red Sea. This story of the Egyptian army destroyed is given added dimension as Moses reminds them of the judgment of those who rebelled against Moses and Aaron when the ground opened up. The story of waters miraculously separated and then brought back together to crush the enemy is paired with a story of the insiders who forgot their own identity and were swallowed up not by waves crashing over them but by the ground opening up under them. God's mighty hand to save is also the mighty judge. Eat this story.

Later Joshua, the new Moses, will tell these people a similar story as they settle into the promised land and as Joshua nears the end of his life. In Joshua 24, the people gather together for a covenant renewal. There God uses Joshua to remind them of this central story of God's might: "When I brought your ancestors out of Egypt, you came to the sea; and the Egyptians pursued your ancestors with chariots and horsemen to the Red Sea. When they cried out to the LORD, he put darkness between you and the Egyptians, and made the sea come upon them and cover them; and your eyes saw what I did to Egypt" (24:6–7 NRSV). This retelling of the Red Sea story serves as part of the lead-up to the central choice Joshua poses to the people at this covenant renewal: "Choose this day whom you will serve" (24:15). The use of narrative reminds the people not only of what God has done in the past but of the God they serve (or reject) today. I am reminded of the way that foundational stories continue to work in this way, linking together the past and the present. For example, consider the retelling of the Last Supper in the Eucharistic prayer: "On the night in which he was betrayed, Jesus took bread . . ." This story is given to us in the Gospels and then retold by Paul in 1 Corinthians 11:23–26. The invitation to the Eucharist itself involves a retelling, a remembrance both of what God has done in Jesus Christ and of what God continues to do in this present moment.

The story of the Egyptian chariots and the Red Sea also sits at the heart of Psalm 136, a psalm that retells the great wonder that God liberates an oppressed people from enslavement and brings them into a rich heritage. The psalmist reflects on the fact that the same God that rules over the heavens and created the earth also made a way out of enslavement for his people (v. 11), made a way through the Red Sea (vv. 13–14), and "overthrew Pharaoh and his army in the Red Sea" (v. 15 NRSV). The refrain throughout this psalm, serving as the second half of each verse, is that God's *hesed* (faithfulness, loving-kindness, loyalty, steadfast love) continues forever. The chariots of Pharaoh collapse under the waves of the Red Sea, speaking not only of God's judgment but also of his mighty hand to save. The same God who created all that exists also calls this people as his own. Remember who you are, ancient Israel. Eat this story.

This mighty hand to save is clearly seen in Isaiah's message to the exilic community. In the same chapter where he speaks of the remnant returning home from exile as a kind of second exodus event, Isaiah reminds his audience of the Red Sea as he speaks about God bringing back a remnant from Assyria:

> And the Lord will *utterly destroy*
> *the tongue of the sea of Egypt;*
> and will *wave his hand over the River*
> with his scorching wind;
> and will split it into seven channels,
> and *make a way to cross on foot*;
> so there shall be *a highway from Assyria*
> for the remnant that is left of his people,
> as there was for Israel
> when they came up from the land of Egypt. (Isa. 11:15–16 NRSV)

The words about crossing the Red Sea are spoken of in a poetic tenor, as you can see in the italicized phrases above. In a similar way to how he uses the word "remnant," Isaiah takes the older exodus story and offers a refreshed telling of God's past deliverance. This retelling brings with it a reminder that what God did back then, God will do once again. God remains both the master of all creation—wind, sea, river, and desert—and the God over ancient Israel.

Manna from the Heavens

> Remember the long way that the Lord your God has led you these forty years in the wilderness, in order to humble you, testing you to know what was in your heart, whether or not you would keep his commandments. He humbled you by letting you hunger, then by feeding you with manna, with which neither you nor your ancestors were acquainted, in order to make you understand that one does not live by bread alone, but by every word that comes from the mouth of the Lord. The clothes on your back did not wear out and your feet did not swell these forty years. (Deut. 8:2–4 NRSV)

In Exodus, we are told that just after God's mighty acts at the Red Sea, the Israelites enter into the wilderness where God provides them water to drink from freshwater springs and offers them shade under a forest of palm trees (Exod. 15:22–27). God then responds to the ensuing complaints of the people that they will starve by promising bread from the heavens that will appear every morning for six days, with an abundance on the sixth day to provide for the seventh day, the day of rest (Exod. 16). Moses reminds the people in Deuteronomy 8:3 that God fed them with manna so that they would "understand that one does not live by bread alone, but by every word that comes from the mouth of the Lord" (NRSV). God will continue to do this work of provision in the promised land if they remember that God is the source of the land's goodness and of the people's abundance. Moses uses a story recollected to remind the Israelites not only that God has provided thus far, but that all goodness in the future comes from God alone. This knowledge is demonstrated by the people through their faithfulness to the Law, their love of God and neighbor, and the way they continue to call to mind these central stories of identity. Forgetfulness leads to waywardness; remembrance leads to continued blessing.

Psalm 78 is a postexilic psalm, which speaks of God's great acts for ancient Israel and their apostasy that led to judgment. This psalm echoes Deuteronomy in retelling God's saving work among the people of God. It is unsurprising, in light of the emphasis on the Passover story and echoes of

Deuteronomy, that Psalm 78 plays a central role in the Jewish observance of the Passover to this day. Psalm 78 begins:

> Give ear, O my people, to my teaching;
>   incline your ears to the words of my mouth.
> I will open my mouth in a parable;
>   I will utter dark sayings from of old,
> things that we have heard and known,
>   that our ancestors have told us.
> We will not hide them from their children;
>   we will tell to the coming generation
> the glorious deeds of the LORD, and his might,
>   and the wonders that he has done. (vv. 1–4 NRSV)

What follows is a poetic retelling of Israel's history from Jacob through to God's judgment in exile. At this song's heart is the image of manna from heaven, which the psalmist uses to put in stark relief God's provision and ancient Israel's apostasy. Similar to Isaiah's recasting of the stories of liberation from Egypt and the remnant returning from exile, the story of God's provision through manna is recast for those about to enter exile. But unlike Isaiah's word of comfort, this recasting is one of judgment:

> Mortals ate the bread of angels;
>   he sent them food in abundance. (78:25 NRSV)

God fed them and provided for them in the wilderness, and yet,

> In spite of all this they still sinned;
>   they did not believe in his wonders. (78:32 NRSV)

The miraculous provisions of manna and quails, of water from rocks, and of full bellies in the midst of a wasteland did not keep God's people from rebelling against God. Eat this story. God's great deeds are tragically and frequently matched by God's people's prodigious failures.

As the remnant of Israel returns from exile to Jerusalem, Nehemiah brings together the postexilic community for a kind of social and religious reset. Nehemiah first gathers the people to read from the Law, confess their own sins and the sins of those who came before them, and worship God.

Then, using a tone similar to that in Deuteronomy, Nehemiah retells the story of their descendants through a prayer to God. Nehemiah's prayer begins, "You are the Lord, you alone . . ." (Neh. 9:6). With this affirmation of the Shema of Deuteronomy 6:4, Nehemiah speaks of the great deeds God has done, from creating the world to the covenant with Abraham to liberation from Egypt. As part of this retelling, Nehemiah speaks of God's provision for the emancipated Israelites: God divided the sea, led the people with pillars of cloud and fire, spoke from the mountain, and gifted the Law (9:9–14). To round out God's miraculous acts of liberating the people and bringing them into the promised land, Nehemiah prays, "For their hunger you gave them bread from heaven, and for their thirst you brought water for them out of the rock" (9:15 NRSV). God not only made a way for his people, across sea and desert, but fed them with food only God can provide. As the remnant community stands amid a city in tatters in the heart of the land God gifted them long ago, a land that they mishandled through waywardness and sin, Nehemiah reminds them of what it means to be the people of God. Nehemiah, amid desolation, instructs the people to eat this story and remember.

In his ministry, Jesus uses the story of God's provision of manna to demonstrate how he himself is part of this great story of God's people. Jesus asks his disciples to recall how their ancestors ate manna during the wilderness wandering. He reminds them, like Moses did, that this bread comes from God and not by any earthly means. Jesus says, I come to you as a gift from God: "I am the bread of life. Whoever comes to me will never be hungry, and whoever believes in me will never be thirsty" (John 6:35 NRSV). Jesus retells this story of manna to both remind them of what God has done and alert them to the new thing God is doing in this present moment. The stories of the past become the interpretive key to understand the incredible reality of Jesus of Nazareth. Like the manna, Jesus also comes as a mysterious and perfect heavenly gift.

The Golden Calf

Even at Horeb you provoked the Lord to wrath, and the Lord was so angry with you that he was ready to destroy you. When I went up the mountain to receive the stone tablets, the tablets of the covenant that the Lord made with you, I remained on the mountain forty days and forty nights; I neither ate bread nor drank water. And the Lord gave me the two stone tablets

> written with the finger of God; on them were all the words that the LORD had spoken to you at the mountain out of the fire on the day of the assembly. At the end of forty days and forty nights the LORD gave me the two stone tablets, the tablets of the covenant. Then the LORD said to me, "Get up, go down quickly from here, for your people whom you have brought from Egypt have acted corruptly. They have been quick to turn from the way that I commanded them; they have cast an image for themselves." Furthermore the LORD said to me, "I have seen that this people is indeed a stubborn people. Let me alone that I may destroy them and blot out their name from under heaven; and I will make of you a nation mightier and more numerous than they."
>
> So I turned and went down from the mountain, while the mountain was ablaze; the two tablets of the covenant were in my two hands. Then I saw that you had indeed sinned against the LORD your God, by casting for yourselves an image of a calf; you had been quick to turn from the way that the LORD had commanded you. So I took hold of the two tablets and flung them from my two hands, smashing them before your eyes. Then I lay prostrate before the LORD as before, forty days and forty nights; I neither ate bread nor drank water, because of all the sin you had committed, provoking the LORD by doing what was evil in his sight. For I was afraid that the anger that the LORD bore against you was so fierce that he would destroy you. But the LORD listened to me that time also. The LORD was so angry with Aaron that he was ready to destroy him, but I interceded also on behalf of Aaron at that same time. Then I took the sinful thing you had made, the calf, and burned it with fire and crushed it, grinding it thoroughly, until it was reduced to dust; and I threw the dust of it into the stream that runs down the mountain. (Deut. 9:8–21 NRSV)

My exploration of some of the central stories of identity in Deuteronomy, those that Moses insists his hearers and following generations must "eat," ends with the story that reminds God's people of their own folly and proclivity to forget. Remember your forgetfulness; remember your folly. We have already seen how this story of forgetfulness shows up in the way some of these earlier stories are retold. Especially in the retelling around the Babylonian exile, we find the miraculous stories of God working among and for his people paired with his people's stubborn refusal to respond with obedience. The story of the golden calf captures their inclination toward forgetfulness and folly. Behind many of the later stumblings of God's people, we hear echoes of just how quickly liberation from enslavement and literal food from heaven were forgotten and replaced with impatient superstition.

In Deuteronomy 9, Moses is primarily concerned with getting the point across that the miraculous signs, wonders, and favor God has shown to ancient Israel are not based on merit. That is, ancient Israel is being ushered into the promised land of milk and honey because of God's love, not as a reward for good behavior. God's favor, not Israel's faithfulness, accounts for God's mighty acts. Moses thinks it important here to remind the people of this foundational truth as they are standing at the threshold of their inheritance: "Know, then, that the Lord your God is not giving you this good land to occupy because of your righteousness; for you are a stubborn people" (Deut. 9:6 NRSV). The story Moses uses to illustrate his point is that of the golden calf.

As Moses communes with God on Mount Sinai, receiving the ten commandments that establish the conditions for God to dwell among ancient Israel, the people create for themselves an idol down below. Moses retells this story in Deuteronomy, of when God gives him the news of idolatry just after receiving the two tablets (Deut. 9:12). God fumes on the mountain; meanwhile, Moses rushes toward the people (9:15–16). You can practically hear the exasperation in Moses's voice as he retells this story.

Von Rad picks up on this tone, noting the pointedness of the way Moses presents the story: "The comprehensive narrative of the events connected with setting up the golden calf is intended to serve a quite definite purpose. Unlike the account given in Ex. 32, the instructive and didactic trend of the description, with its 'Remember and do not forget,' is evident from the start. The Israel which faces its God today with same rebelliousness as it did then must learn from past events and become conscious of its own threatening situation. Without such a powerful intercessor [in Moses] Israel would have been lost even then."[11] Remember, Moses insists, how quick you were to forget what the Lord asked of you. Notably, in this story, not only God's mercy but Moses's role as mediator is central. Moses's retelling of the story is an intensely personal one. Remember your stubbornness and folly. Remember how I advocated for you and pleaded for mercy. Remember what has been done on your behalf, despite your unwillingness to recognize it. Eat this story.

11. Von Rad, *Deuteronomy*, 77–78.

The account of the golden calf continues to show up in Scripture, often referred to as "the calf at Horeb" to reinforce to its audience that this story is not just about any molten idol (a common form of ancient Near East religious practice). Instead, this is a calf at Horeb in the wilderness, which was crafted as God was working miracles among his people. The story shows up again in Nehemiah's prayer during the communal confession: "But you are a God ready to forgive, gracious and merciful, slow to anger and abounding in steadfast love, and you did not forsake them. Even when they had cast an image of a calf for themselves and said, 'This is your God who brought you up out of Egypt,' and had committed great blasphemies, you in your great mercies did not forsake them in the wilderness" (Neh. 9:17–19 NRSV). And, again, when Stephen stands before the Sanhedrin in Acts: "Our ancestors were unwilling to obey [Moses]; instead they pushed him aside, and in their hearts they turned back to Egypt, saying to Aaron, 'Make gods for us who will lead the way for us; as for this Moses who led us out from the land of Egypt, we do not know what has happened to him.' At that time they made a calf, offered a sacrifice to the idol, and reveled in the work of their hands" (Acts 7:39–41 NRSV). In the mouths of both Nehemiah and Stephen, we hear the call to remember this story and not repeat the mistakes of the past.

In Psalm 106, we find a reflection on ancient Israel's idolatry in the context of an extended confession. This confession is most likely dated to the Second Temple era, the time of Nehemiah, as the exilic remnant returns to Jerusalem to piece back together the ruins. John Goldingay captures the essence of this era and this psalm with the summary that "all was not well."[12] While the preceding psalm extols God's great acts among ancient Israel, Psalm 106 places at the forefront a recounting of the Israelites' forgetfulness, sin, and hypocrisy. Near the center of this recital of the people's failing we find the story of the golden calf:

> They made a calf at Horeb
>   and worshiped a cast image.
> They exchanged the glory of God
>   for the image of an ox that eats grass.
> They forgot God, their Savior,
>   who had done great things in Egypt,

12. Goldingay, *Psalms*, 223.

wondrous works in the land of Ham,
and awesome deeds by the Red Sea.
Therefore he said he would destroy them—
had not Moses, his chosen one,
stood in the breach before him,
to turn away his wrath from destroying them. (Ps. 106:19–23 NRSV)

You can hear the exasperation of Moses, of the prophets, of Stephen before the Sanhedrin, of Paul in writing to the early churches in this poetic vexation: "They exchanged the glory of God for the image of an ox that eats grass."

I often can relate to Moses's frustration when reading about how quickly and often ancient Israel forgets what they have been told to remember (I, of course, would never be so forgetful!). I am reminded of a recent Bible study at my church where we were discussing the story of the rich young ruler recounted in three of the four Gospels (Matt. 19:16–30; Mark 10:17–31; Luke 18:18–30). To many in the room, Jesus's declaration that it is easier for a camel to go through the eye of a needle than for a rich man to enter God's kingdom sounds like a judgment about the danger of riches—which it is. But one parishioner shifted the angle of the story by pointing out that Jesus simply wanted what was best for this young man. In love, Jesus lamented that this young man was missing out on the sweet riches of God.

This shift in focus reminds me of what the psalmist does in Psalm 106, when he explains that Israel has traded the glory of God, Creator and sustainer of all things, for a creature that chews the cud. We hear this pathetic trade echoed at the start of Romans in a more straightforward nature: "They are without excuse; for though they knew God, they did not honor him as God or give thanks to him, but they became futile in their thinking, and their senseless minds were darkened" (Rom. 1:20–21 NRSV).

It is easy, at least for me, to read these kinds of passages as pure condemnation, but the parishioner's comments about the rich young ruler found their way into my thinking about how God's people did and continue to miss the gracious gifts before them. The frustration in the mouths of psalmists, prophets, martyrs, and apostles for the pathetic trade speaks not only to God's frustration but to God's love for his people and his desire for them to have what is best for them—that they be fruitful, delight in the world God has made, thrive, and be known for how their love for God cultivates communities of love for their neighbor. Remember the golden calf. Remember the pathetic trade. Eat this story.

Conclusion

Moses's retelling of central stories of identity leads us to a final reflection on the invitation in the book of Deuteronomy. Reading through Deuteronomy reminds us of God's great love. Moses instructs these people who are on the precipice of a major life change to remember who they are: the beloved and chosen people of God, the ones gifted with an unmerited but very real and liberating identity as the people of God, and the ones who, despite this good gift, continue to do what is contrary to their own well-being. Moses retells the stories of the past not only as a reminder of the paths subsequent generations have trod but as an invitation to his present audience to remember who they are and what God has done on their behalf. This invitation is one of both hope and warning. It is an invitation we find in the retelling of these central stories to subsequent generations of ancient Israel and to the early Christian community. Deuteronomy is an invitation to us today to remember. It is an invitation to eat these stories, both to know the good news of God's love for us and to be warned of our proclivity to not love ourselves well by not walking in the way God has set before us.

EPILOGUE

The conviction that reading not only informs but transforms readers stands at the heart of this book's invitation to read the stories of the Pentateuch. I believe this transformation is why the critique of certain critical methods of reading Scripture resonated so deeply with me in my early scholarly days of delving into the wide and contentious world of biblical interpretation. At the same time, the beauty of biblical Hebrew storytelling expanded my path as I traversed the stories of the Old Testament. Some of the more flippant language used in circles of spiritual or theological interpretation suggests that the artistry of the stories is merely a husk that must be stripped away to get to a spiritual kernel. Much like the incarnate God-Man, the text and the spirit (the husk and the kernel) cannot be separated. Form and content are inextricably linked.

The transformative power of reading also suggests that I don't know everything already. I do not come to Scripture knowing what it should or could say to me. This recognition of learning something new, of meeting God in a new way through these stories of faithfulness, struggle, missteps, and grace, cultivates a posture of humility. If I believe that I have something to learn from the text that I do not already know, then the invitation also can become communal. I look to other pilgrims on this journey who seek to be transformed through their reading. On my own journey of accepting this invitation, one of the greatest discoveries has been that I can journey with faithful seekers across time, cultures, and backgrounds. The disposition of discovery and surprise generates a more hospitable posture to those readers, who can help me see with new eyes.

This posture of reading also cultivates an openness to the text, an openness to allowing it to speak to us in ways that may surprise, delight, or unsettle us. Recall Gadamer's insistence that the relationship between reader and text is more of a conversation than a dissection. If I were to sit down with a friend for coffee, already confident that I know why we're having a chat or firmly set on what I want to get out of the conversation, I imagine that my friend would not be as keen to have coffee with me again. I also might miss out on the surprising news she wanted to tell me that I couldn't have anticipated because I did not allow space for more vulnerability. We come to a text like the Pentateuch receptive and ready to discover something new—about the text or ourselves—even in the most well-worn stories of bygone Sunday school lessons.

The five features we discussed in this book—brevity, pacing, characterization, complexity, and the grotesque—mark artistry available to us in biblical Hebrew narrative. A story of only a couple paragraphs, even of only a few lines, while diminutive in size speaks of grand events like wrestling with angels or even the creation of the entire world. Biblical Hebrew storytelling without all the narrative cues of punctuation marks and the conjunction "and" doing heavy lifting is foreign not only to English but to modern language more generally. This lack of cues leads to a very different feel for the pacing and sequencing of events. In the Pentateuch, we are rarely told anything about a figure's appearance, personal preferences, or interior life. Instead, we come to know characters through the bluntness of narrative action and dialogue. The necessarily inferential task of coming to know the key figures of the Pentateuch requires an attentiveness to interpersonal dynamics, the infrequently offered extra details, and narrative cues buried within narrative action and dialogue. And while it is only one of the many subfeatures of biblical narrative, the presence of the grotesque in the Pentateuch serves as an entry into the big questions of biblical narrative, questions that can only be asked once we come to appreciate the artistry in the distorted, cringe-worthy, disgusting, and strange.

This book does not encompass all that it means to be invited into the artistry of biblical narrative. What I offered here is a *curated* look at the stories of the Pentateuch. I attend to both the significant and distinct narrative features (brevity, pacing, characterization) and to examples of how to delve more deeply into even the most familiar stories through complexity and the grotesque. We are just beginning to plumb the depths of the invitation we found in the older testament.

I like to think of cultivating this posture toward the text as a kind of attunement to the artistry of biblical narrative. Attunement comes through both knowledge of narrative features and exposure to those features in practice. The more we attend to the artistry of these ancient stories, the more attuned we will be to discovering something new and fresh in Scripture. This attunement keeps Scripture's ability to speak to us evergreen, never mastered and never exhausted. My hope is that by attending to the artistry of the stories that make up the Pentateuch we can become both more attuned to and appreciative of the ways biblical stories function nondidactically. That is, these stories are told not simply to get a point across but to help us delve into the beauty and complexity of a story of the human in communion with Creator God, a communion impossible except for by the grace of God.

The artistry of the first five books extends into the whole of Scripture, from the accounts of the entrance into the land of promise, to the establishment of ancient Israel's first kings, to the division of that nation into two nations, which led ancient Israel deeper and deeper into forgetting what it means to be God's own. The artistry continues in the poetry of the psalmists, the prophetic oracles, and the wisdom sayings that make up the latter half of the Old Testament. And in the intertestamental period we find stories of God's miraculous provision and of human heroism and faithfulness. Jesus's most effective and profound mode of communicating the good news of the kingdom came through the artistry of parables, sermons, and object lessons. Maybe we are too quick to excavate meaning from Scripture and too slow to attend to the quiet and careful artistic invitation of stories, poems, songs, and parables.

I have found that accepting the invitation of the first five books has rippled out not only into my reading of Scripture but into the wider world of reading (and of listening). Cultivating an attunement to the artistry in biblical Hebrew narrative has also cultivated an attunement more broadly to listen, to wonder, to wander, and to be ready discover something new in texts, in neighbors, and in ourselves.

BIBLIOGRAPHY

Abbott, H. Porter. *The Cambridge Introduction to Narrative*. Cambridge: Cambridge University Press, 2002.

Alter, Robert. *The Art of Bible Translation*. Princeton: Princeton University Press, 2019.

———. *The Art of Biblical Narrative*. Rev. ed. New York: Basic Books, 2011.

———. *The Art of Biblical Poetry*. Rev. ed. New York: Basic Books, 2011.

———. *The Five Books of Moses: A Translation with Commentary*. New York: Norton, 2008.

———. *The Hebrew Bible: A Translation with Commentary*. Vol. 1, *The Five Books of Moses: Torah*. New York: Norton, 2019.

———. *Pen of Iron: American Prose and the King James Bible*. Princeton: Princeton University Press, 2010.

Alter, Robert, and Frank Kermode, eds. *The Literary Guide to the Bible*. Cambridge, MA: Belknap, 1990.

Aristotle. *Poetics: With the "Tractatus Coislinianus," Reconstruction of "Poetics II," and the Fragments of the "On Poets."* Translated by Richard Janko. 3rd ed. Indianapolis: Hackett, 1987.

Auerbach, Erich. *Mimesis: The Representation of Reality in Western Literature*. 50th anniv. ed. Princeton: Princeton University Press, 2013. Originally published 1953.

Azriel, Yakov. "Rebecca and Esau." *Nashim: A Journal of Jewish Women's Studies and Gender Issues*, no. 8 (2004): 245.

Bal, Mieke. *Narratology: Introduction to the Theory of Narrative*. 3rd ed. Toronto: University of Toronto Press, 2000.

Bar-Efrat, Shimon. *Narrative Art in the Bible*. London: Bloomsbury T&T Clark, 2004.

Bellinger, W. H. *Introducing Old Testament Theology: Creation, Covenant, and Prophecy in the Divine-Human Relationship*. Grand Rapids: Baker Academic, 2022.

Berlin, Adele. *Poetics and Interpretation of Biblical Narrative*. Winona Lake, IN: Eisenbrauns, 1994.

Bibb, Bryan D. *Ritual Words and Narrative Worlds in the Book of Leviticus*. Library of Hebrew Bible / Old Testament Studies 480. New York: T&T Clark, 2009.

Book of Common Prayer, The. New York: Church Hymnal Corporation, 1979.

Brueggemann, Walter. *Genesis*. Interpretation: A Bible Commentary for Teaching and Preaching. Atlanta: John Knox, 1986.

———. *Theology of the Old Testament: Testimony, Dispute, Advocacy*. Minneapolis: Fortress, 2005.

Childs, Brevard S. *Introduction to the Old Testament as Scripture*. Philadelphia: Fortress, 1979.

Coogan, Michael D. *A Reader of Ancient Near Eastern Texts: Sources for the Study of the Old Testament*. Oxford: Oxford University Press, 2012.

Cotter, David W. *Genesis*. Collegeville, MN: Liturgical Press, 2003.

Cross, Frank Moore. *Canaanite Myth and Hebrew Epic: Essays in the History of the Religion of Israel*. Cambridge, MA: Harvard University Press, 1973.

Davis, Ellen F. *Getting Involved with God: Rediscovering the Old Testament*. Cambridge, MA: Cowley, 2001.

Fishbane, Michael. *Biblical Text and Texture: A Literary Reading of Selected Texts*. Oxford: Oneworld, 1998.

Fokkelman, J. P. "Genesis." In *The Literary Guide to the Bible*, edited by Robert Alter and Frank Kermode, 36–55. Cambridge, MA: Belknap, 1990.

———. *Reading Biblical Poetry: An Introduction*. Louisville: Westminster John Knox, 2001.

———. Review of *The Art of Biblical Narrative*, by Robert Alter. *Journal of Biblical Literature* 102, no. 3 (1983): 441–42.

Fretheim, Terence E. *Exodus*. Interpretation: A Bible Commentary for Teaching and Preaching. Louisville: Westminster John Knox, 1991.

Friedman, Richard Elliot. *The Bible with Sources Revealed*. San Francisco: HarperOne, 2005.

Gadamer, Hans-Georg. *Truth and Method*. Translated by J. Weinsheimer and D. G. Marshall. 2nd rev. ed. New York: Continuum, 2004.

Gafney, Wilda C. *Womanist Midrash: A Reintroduction to the Women of the Torah and the Throne*. Louisville: Westminster John Knox, 2017.

Gerstenberger, Erhard S. *Leviticus: A Commentary*. Old Testament Library. Louisville: Westminster John Knox, 1996.

Gignilliat, Mark S. *Reading Scripture Canonically: Theological Instincts for Old Testament Interpretation*. Grand Rapids: Baker Academic, 2019.

Goldingay, John. *Psalms*. Vol. 3, *Psalms 90–150*. Baker Commentary on the Old Testament Wisdom and Psalms. Grand Rapids: Baker Academic, 2008.

Hays, Rebecca W. Poe. *The Function of Story in the Hebrew Psalter*. Lanham, MD: Lexington Books / Fortress Academic, 2021.

———. "Trauma, Remembrance, and Healing: The Meeting of Wisdom and History in Psalm 78." *Journal for the Study of the Old Testament* 41, no. 2 (2016): 183–204.

Hösle, V. "Hermenuetics." In *The Princeton Encyclopedia of Poetry and Poetics*, edited by Roland, Stephen Cushman, Clare Cavanagh, Jahan Ramazani, Paul Rouzer, Harris Feinsod, David Marno, and Alexandra Slessarev, 592–651. 4th ed. Princeton: Princeton University Press, 2012.

International Council on Biblical Inerrancy. *The Chicago Statement on Biblical Hermeneutics*. Oakland: The Council, 1982.

———. *The Chicago Statement on Biblical Inerrancy*. Oakland: The Council, 1978.

Iser, Wolfgang. *The Act of Reading: A Theory of Aesthetic Response*. Baltimore: Johns Hopkins University Press, 1980.

Iser, Wolfgang, Norman N. Holland, and Wayne C. Booth. "Interview: Wolfgang Iser." *Diacritics* 10, no. 2 (1980): 57–74.

Kawashima, Robert S. *Biblical Narrative and the Death of the Rhapsode*. Bloomington: Indiana University Press, 2004.

Kierkegaard, Søren. *Fear and Trembling and the Sickness unto Death*. Princeton Princeton University Press, 1941.

Koehler, L., W. Baumgartner, and J. J. Stamm. *The Hebrew and Aramaic Lexicon of the Old Testament*. Translated and edited under the supervision of M. E. J. Richardson. 4 vols. Leiden: Brill, 1994–99.

Legaspi, Michael C. *The Death of Scripture and the Rise of Biblical Studies*. Oxford: Oxford University Press, 2011.

Levin, Menashe. "Isaac Blesses Jacob and Esau, a Story." *The Literary Review* 1 (1958): 309–15.

Long, V. Philips. *The Art of Biblical History*. Grand Rapids: Zondervan, 1994.

Louth, Andrew. *Discerning the Mystery: An Essay on the Nature of Theology*. Oxford: Oxford University Press, 1990.

Lowth, Robert. *De Sacra Poesi Hebræorum: Prælectiones Academiæ Oxonii Habitæ*. Oxford: Oxonii, 1753.

McGinnis, Claire Mathews. "The Hardening of Pharaoh's Heart in Christian and Jewish Interpretation." *Journal of Theological Interpretation* 6, no. 1 (2012): 43–64.

Milgrom, Jacob. *The JPS Torah Commentary: Numbers*. Philadelphia: Jewish Publication Society, 2003.

———. *Leviticus 1–16: A New Translation with Introduction and Commentary*. Anchor Bible. New York: Doubleday, 1991.

Noth, Martin. *Leviticus: A Commentary*. Translated by J. E. Anderson. The Old Testament Library. Philadelphia: Westminster, 1965.

———. *Numbers: A Commentary*. Translated by James D. Martin. The Old Testament Library. Philadelphia: Westminster, 1968.

O'Connor, Flannery. *The Habit of Being: Letters of Flannery O'Connor*. Edited by Sally Fitzgerald. Reprint ed. New York: Farrar, Straus & Giroux, 1988.

———. *Mystery and Manners: Occasional Prose*. Edited by Sally Fitzgerald and Robert Fitzgerald. New York: Farrar, Straus and Giroux, 1970.

Olson, Dennis T. *Numbers*. Interpretation: A Bible Commentary for Teaching and Preaching. Louisville: Westminster John Knox, 2012.

Origen. *On First Principles*. Translated by John Behr. Oxford Early Christian Texts. Oxford: Oxford University Press, 2018.

Peterson, Eugene H. *Eat This Book: A Conversation in the Art of Spiritual Reading*. Grand Rapids: Eerdmans, 2006.

Prince, Gerald. *A Dictionary of Narratology*. Rev. ed. Lincoln: University of Nebraska Press, 2003.

Rimmon-Kenan, Shlomith. *Narrative Fiction: Contemporary Poetics*. London: Methuen, 1983.

Saffitz, Claire. *Dessert Person: Recipes and Guidance for Baking with Confidence*. New York: Clarkson Potter, 2020.

Sanders, Seth L. *The Invention of Hebrew*. Chicago: University of Illinois Press, 2009.

Sarna, Nahum M. *The JPS Torah Commentary: Genesis*. Philadelphia: Jewish Publication Society, 2001.

Smith, Craig A. "Reinstating Isaac: The Centrality of Abraham's Son in the 'Jacob-Esau' Narrative of Genesis 27." *Biblical Theology Bulletin* 31 (2001): 130–34.

Smith, Mark S. "Biblical Narrative between Ugaritic and Akkadian Literature—Part I: Ugarit and the Hebrew Bible; Consideration of Comparative Research." *Revue Biblique* 114, no. 1 (2007): 5–29.

———. "Biblical Narrative between Ugaritic and Akkadian Literature—Part II: Mesopotamian Impact on Biblical Narrative." *Revue Biblique* 114, no. 2 (2007): 189–207.

Sonderegger, Katherine. *The Doctrine of the Holy Trinity: Processions and Persons*. Vol. 2 of *Systematic Theology*. Minneapolis: Fortress, 2020.

Steiner, Richard C. (Richard Cecil). "Does the Biblical Hebrew Conjunction -ו Have Many Meanings, One Meaning, or No Meaning at All?" *Journal of Biblical Literature* 119, no. 2 (2000): 249–67.

Sternberg, Meir. *The Poetics of Biblical Narrative: Ideological Literature and the Drama of Reading*. Bloomington: Indiana University Press, 1987.

Talmon, Shemaryahu. "The 'Comparative Method' in Biblical Interpretation—Principles and Problems." In *Congress Volume Göttingen 1977*, edited by John Emerton, 320–56. Vetus Testamentum, Supplements 29. Leiden: Brill, 1978.

Tolkien, J. R. R. *The Lord of the Rings*. 50th anniv. ed. Boston: Morrow, 2005.

———. "On Fairy-Stories." In *The Tolkien Reader*, 33–99. New York: Ballantine Books, 1986.

Toombs, Rachel. *Flannery O'Connor and Stylistic Asceticism*. Eugene, OR: Pickwick, 2022.

Tutu, Desmond M. *Children of God Storybook Bible*. Grand Rapids: Zonderkidz, 2010.

Vanhoozer, Kevin J. *Is There a Meaning in This Text? The Bible, the Reader, and the Morality of Literary Knowledge*. Grand Rapids: Zondervan Academic, 2009.

von Rad, Gerhard. *Deuteronomy*. Translated by Dorothea Barton. Philadelphia: Westminster, 1966.

Waltke, Bruce K., and Michael P. O'Connor. *Introduction to Biblical Hebrew Syntax*. Winona Lake, IN: Eisenbrauns, 1990.

Walton, John H. *Ancient Near Eastern Thought and the Old Testament*. Grand Rapids: Baker Academic, 2006.

———. *The Lost World of Genesis One: Ancient Cosmology and the Origins Debate*. Downers Grove, IL: IVP Academic, 2010.

West, Travis. *Biblical Hebrew: An Interactive Approach*. Wilmore, KY: GlossaHouse, 2016.

Westphal, Merold. *Whose Community? Which Interpretation? Philosophical Hermeneutics for the Church*. Grand Rapids: Baker Academic, 2009.

Williams, Delores S. *Sisters in the Wilderness: The Challenge of Womanist God*. Anniv. ed. Maryknoll, NY: Orbis Books, 2013.

Williams, Rowan. *The Edge of Words: God and the Habits of Language*. London: Bloomsbury Academic, 2014.

SCRIPTURE INDEX

Old Testament

Genesis

Exodus

Leviticus

Numbers

SUBJECT INDEX